Client
Issues
in Counselling
and Psychotherapy

SAGE has been part of the global academic community since 1965, supporting high quality research and learning that transforms society and our understanding of individuals, groups, and cultures. SAGE is the independent, innovative, natural home for authors, editors and societies who share our commitment and passion for the social sciences.

Find out more at: **www.sagepublications.com**

Client Issues
in Counselling
and Psychotherapy

Edited by

Janet Tolan and
Paul Wilkins

Los Angeles | London | New Delhi
Singapore | Washington DC

First published 2012

SAGE Publications Ltd
1 Oliver's Yard
55 City Road
London EC1Y 1SP

SAGE Publications Inc.
2455 Teller Road
Thousand Oaks, California 91320

SAGE Publications India Pvt Ltd
B 1/I 1 Mohan Cooperative Industrial Area
Mathura Road
New Delhi 110 044

SAGE Publications Asia-Pacific Pte Ltd
33 Pekin Street #02-01
Far East Square
Singapore 048763

Library of Congress Control Number: 2011927511

British Library Cataloguing in Publication data

A catalogue record for this book is available from the British Library

ISBN 978-1-84860-026-3
ISBN 978-1-84860-027-0 (pbk)

Typeset by C&M Digitals (P) Ltd, Chennai, India
Printed and bound by CPI Group (UK) Ltd, Croydon, CR0 4YY
Printed on paper from sustainable resources

CONTENTS

r

ABOUT THE EDITORS AND AUTHORS

Janet Tolan has worked in counselling and psychotherapy since 1979, as a volunteer, as a full-time counsellor, as Leader of Counselling courses at City College, Manchester and as head of the Masters Programme at Liverpool John Moores University. She has also worked in Management Development and Team Development for organisations as diverse as Manchester Airport and Salford Social Services. She now has a small private practice, working with individuals, couples, groups and teams – and also enjoys dancing salsa and singing jazz.

Paul Wilkins was an academic for twenty years and is now a free agent. He continues to write papers, chapters and books, speak at national and international events and practice as a therapist, supervisor and consultant. His books include *Person-Centred Therapy in Focus, Person-Centred Therapy: 100 Key Points* and (with Pete Sanders) *First Steps in Practitioner Research*. Paul values and enjoys his roles as Dad and Granddad, loves good food and wine, music of many kinds, travel and being out and about in the countryside. His friends and family are even more important to him than the person-centred approach!

Richard Bryant-Jefferies has several years of experience of working as a person-centred therapist and supervisor in the NHS in both primary care and private practice. He also has eight years of experience as a primary care liaison alcohol counsellor and supervisor within substance misuse services. He has authored twenty-three books, fiction and non-fiction, addressing a range of specialist counselling themes, including gambling, alcohol and drug use, sexual abuse, self-harm, eating disorders, trauma, disability, mental health and working with young people (see www.richardbj.co.uk). Richard has a regular column on the British Association for Counselling and Psychotherapy (BACP) website exploring supervision issues. Since 2006, Richard has worked in the rich and rewarding field of equality and diversity at an NHS Trust in London.

Rose Cameron has been practising as a person-centred counsellor since 1990. She has worked in the voluntary and statutory sectors as well as in private practice. Her interest in drug and alcohol issues began when she worked in Europe's first 'wet house' for crude-spirit drinkers. She has also worked in drug and alcohol rehabs, where she became aware of the need for self-injury to be better understood. She lives in Scotland and is studying for a PhD at the University of Edinburgh.

Barbara Douglas is a chartered psychologist, registered counselling psychologist and medical historian. She currently works as Registrar for the British Psychological Society's Qualification in Counselling Psychology and in private practice and is an honorary fellow of the University of Exeter. Barbara is Chair of the Division of Counselling Psychology and Chair Elect of the Representative Council of the British Psychological Society. Barbara was formerly Senior Lecturer in Counselling Psychology at the University of the West of England and prior to that was Director of the North West Centre for Eating Disorders, in association with Stockport Primary Care Trust. She is co-editor of the third edition of the *Sage Handbook of Counselling Psychology* and has particular interest in the histories of both psychology and psychiatry.

Sheila Haugh, formerly a senior lecturer in psychotherapy at Leeds Metropolitan University and an honorary psychotherapist with Leeds Psychological Services, has worked as a person-centred practitioner for over thirty years. She is a board member of the World Association for Person-Centred and Experiential Psychotherapy and Counselling, a member of the editorial boards of *Person-Centred and Experiential Psychotherapies* and the *Person-Centered Journal* and the academic editor of *Person-Centred Quarterly*. More recently she has been working in the Czech Republic with the senior management teams of international companies as a consultant and coach.

Jane Power works in private practice as a psychotherapist, supervisor and employee assistance counsellor in West Yorkshire and South Manchester. She facilitated community education groups during the 1980s and in 1986 qualified as a counsellor. Jane gained her MA in 2001, researching into the experiences of being a supervisee. She has Senior Accredited status with BACP as a psychotherapist and supervisor. Jane worked on several Diploma courses and for eight years ran a staff counselling service in the NHS. She has worked with people affected by trauma and abuse throughout her professional life and is currently developing Lifespan Integration therapy.

Kirshen Rundle is a UK-based person-centred therapist. She has an MA in Counselling and is an accredited member of BACP. Her clinical experience has included work with clients from a person-centred counselling agency, an adult male prison and young offenders' institution, a university counselling service and in private practice. She is currently working with clients from an NHS mental health trust and a low-secure psychiatric unit. She is also doing a PhD which is exploring the lived experiences of person-centred therapy for people who hear voices. She has taught an undergraduate seminar group and presents papers at conferences both in the UK and internationally.

Allan Turner (Senior Accredited member of BACP) has been a person-centred counsellor since 1985 and a critical incident debriefer since 1999, when he attended the bombing at the Admiral Duncan pub in London. He has subsequently attended numerous public transport accidents and hundreds of bank raids – many armed. He is Clinical Director of Counselling Works, an innovative private counselling agency in Milton Keynes and Bedford. He is interested in areas of therapeutic work that are not usually associated with the person-centred approach. He is a past Chair of the British Association for the Person-Centred Approach and a founder member of the Association for Person-Centred Therapy Scotland (PCT Scotland).

1

INTRODUCTION

PAUL WILKINS AND JANET TOLAN

This book is primarily about how you might work with clients experiencing one or more of a number of life events, emotional reactions to life events or behavioural reactions to life events. Our theoretical and practice stance is person-centred and a good understanding of the theory of person-centred (also known as client-centred) therapy is essential to the work described in this book. In order to set the scene, in this chapter we are going to remind you of some of the fundamentals of person-centred theory and how they relate to practice. However, our reminder is necessarily brief so, at the end of the chapter, we have provided a guide to **Further Reading** for those of you who want to know more.

As we say above, this book translates theory into everyday events as they affect us as people and as we encounter them in the therapy room. Why would someone wreck their own health by eating too much or by overindulging in drugs or alcohol? Why does one person seem to be able to grieve and reach a place of relative calm, where another is pitched into years of emotional pain? How does childhood abuse affect the adult and how can the person-centred therapist help? Each chapter is written by an experienced practitioner who is able to convey *how it actually is* in the therapy room and relate this to person-centred theory.

In the person-centred tradition different individuals respond differently to each experience they may have, in accordance with their self-structure, so that we cannot make definite statements along the lines of: *if A happens then people will feel B and C*. We are even rather wary of statements like *most people* will feel B and C because we have seen how tentative statements like *Following a bereavement, a specific sample of people seemed to go through these stages* have become *There are five stages of grieving*. However, there is a clear need for us to show how the person-centred theoretical framework is applied to a range of presenting issues that are common in the therapy room.

Presenting Issues

When a client first approaches a counselling service, we use the term *presenting issue* to indicate that aspect of a client's experience they choose to highlight. However, this term covers a very wide range of experiences. We may call these experiences bereavement, depression, self-harm, sexual abuse, substance use and so on but it is important to recognise that these are a shorthand way of referring to ways of experiencing the world and reacting to life events and that they vary from individual to individual and with time. Also, in practice, these are often interrelated; for example a person may react to a life event that they have experienced (for example, childhood abuse) both emotionally (perhaps by being 'depressed') and behaviourally (for instance, by developing a problem with respect to food). Similarly, a bereaved person might well experience depression or turn to alcohol to numb their pain.

There are three Parts in this book. Part 1 illustrates how a client may present with a story relating to an experienced life event. Usually this will be something that has received media attention and is considered to be 'big' enough by the clients to warrant their giving it time and paying it attention. In this book, we use loss and bereavement, experiencing traumatising events and childhood sexual abuse as our examples. This list is not exclusive. Again, it is entirely possible – even probable – that a client who comes initially 'suffering from', say, depression will discover their own losses or abuse through the therapeutic process.

Part 2 of the book focuses on psychological and emotional responses to life events. The examples we use are depression, anxiety and 'different realities' – that is, a range of responses that are usually termed 'psychoses' or mental illness. Person-centred theory sees these as the positive attempts of the organism to promote change. Simplistically put, just as a broken leg hurts to alert its owner that it needs attention, so does a wounded psyche.

Part 3 looks at behavioural responses to life events, specifically substance use, difficulties with eating and self-harm. Again, in terms of person-centred theory these behaviours are seen as functional for the organism – to self-soothe, say, or to take control, or to remain part of a drug-based community. This latter point illustrates that although there might be many commonalities within a given subject area, person-centred theory demands that we listen to the individual client – to *their* reasons for being depressed, to *their* reasons for self-harming. Moreover, through this process the client will come to hear their own reasons and grow in self-acceptance.

Person-Centred Theory

Since Rogers and his colleagues began to develop what was then called 'client-centred therapy' (previously 'non-directive therapy') in the 1940s and 1950s, a family of related approaches has been established around the original conceptions. Major branches of this family include focusing, experiential and process-experiential therapies. However, the focus of this book is on what in the UK is normally called 'person-centred therapy' – that is, an approach to therapy that has the non-directive attitude at the centre of theory and practice. Because it focuses on and explores practice, it will be useful to people training as person-centred therapists, to practitioners of the approach and to anyone else who wants an easily accessible sourcebook covering the major aspects of the 'how to' of person-centred therapy.

At the core of person-centred theory is the hypothesis of the *actualising tendency*. This is the drive within us all towards accepting ourselves as we are and the world as it is. Like the plant that will keep on trying to grow no matter how badly it is treated, we are all trying to develop in the best way we can. In many therapies, there is an attempt to seek to diagnose what is wrong with a person and then to fix it. Person-centred theory tells us that people are always doing the best they can in the circumstances in which they find themselves and that the way to understand someone is for therapists to put themselves in the client's shoes (i.e. to experience the client's world *as if* it were their own). Moreover, the very act of empathising in this way becomes part of the healing process. It is because of the actualising tendency that the therapist's job is to support the growth of the individual no matter what direction that growth may take, and so another concept central to person-centred therapy is *the non-directive attitude*.

However, this is a book about presenting issues. How does the theory 'fit' with something like bereavement – and what practice follows from this? It is impossible as a therapist to separate the person (or client) from what they are going through. Our theory explains how and why the self-structure has developed as it is in each individual and how some – or much – of this will be out of the individual's awareness. So, when people receive psychological blows, they will each respond according to their self-structure. In dealing with the event in a therapeutic setting, each of them will probably become aware of some of those elements of the self-structure that are less functional in the current situation – and possibly in life generally. In the example of bereavement, one client may come to realise that she is driven to care for others and is not able to accept care for herself; another may realise that expressing grief is, in his own eyes, fundamentally unmanly; yet another may question his belief in a loving deity. So the basic work of person-centred therapeutic endeavour – a greater integration of self-structure and experience and hence a reduction in anxiety and distress – is undertaken.

Our theory tells us that people seek therapeutic help when difficult and uncomfortable emotions are experienced strongly or chronically.

The second of Rogers' necessary and sufficient conditions specifically requires that the client be *vulnerable or anxious*. This is the organism's way of prompting us to pay attention to ourselves (just as a physical pain or ache prompts us to go to the doctor). With some clients, the prompt will be an event like a mugging or being made redundant, with others it will be a longstanding feeling that does not go away such as anxiety or depression. Because each client is unique, we need a thorough grounding in our fundamental theory of personality development and therapeutic change in addition to an understanding of the common features of presenting issues such as abuse, bereavement or depression. We also need the sensitivity and ability to combine these with a personal response to the person with whom we are working, remembering that it is the client not theory that is at the centre of the process.

Person-Centred Personality Theory

The originator of what was then usually known as client-centred therapy, Carl Rogers, wrote the following about his theory of personality (Rogers, 1951: 532):

> This theory is basically phenomenological in character, and relies heavily on the concept of the self as an explanatory construct. It pictures the end-point of personality development as being a basic congruence between the phenomenal field of experience and the conceptual structure of the self – a situation which, if achieved, would represent freedom from internal strain and anxiety, and freedom from potential strain; which would represent the maximum in realistically oriented adaptation; which would mean the establishment of an individualized value system having considerable identity with the value system of any other equally well-adjusted member of the human race.

The 'Nineteen Propositions' detailed in Rogers (1951: 483–522) and the classic paper also by Rogers (1959) provide an elegant statement of a theory of personality consistent with person-centred concepts of change (Wilkins, 2010: 31). In these works Rogers demonstrates the person-centred view of the person as continually in process – that is, personality as fluid, not fixed. Explicit in this theory is that harmful and/or inhibiting early experiences give rise to distortions and denial of experience and that these give rise to emotional or psychological distress. However, people have the potential to accept their experiences into awareness and to move towards being 'fully functioning'.

Rogers himself refined and restated his person-centred theory of personality, and always made it clear that he saw theory as something to be held tentatively and continually tested against practice. In the light of this encouragement towards inquisitiveness, many practitioners and writers have further explored and developed his theoretical ideas.

Drawing together threads from Rogers' theoretical statements, Sanders (2006: 21–4) characterises person-centred personality theory as:

- **A phenomenological theory:** it emphasises the subjective, experiential world of the individual.
- **A perceptual theory:** because an individual's reality is based on his or her perception of the world, then a change in perception leads to a change in experience and behaviour.
- **A humanistic theory:** it is rooted in a naturalistic philosophy that (p. 23) 'relies primarily on reason and science, democracy and human compassion'.
- **A holistic theory:** the organism is central – human beings are (more than?) the sum total of their parts.
- **A fulfilment of potential, growth-oriented theory:** the person-centred metaphor for recovery is not 'cure' or 'mending' or 'reprogramming' but of growth or development to a new way of being.
- **A process theory:** neither personality nor self are fixed 'things', rather, being human is a process, not a state.

Self-Structure, Self-Concept and Organismic Experiencing

Central to person-centred theory is the concept of the 'organism', that is, the whole person comprising a number of subsystems, including biochemical, physiological, perceptual, emotional, behavioural and relational systems. This organism simply experiences the world. In order to make sense of that experience, human beings develop a 'self'.

While it is acknowledged that 'self' is a process, fluid rather than fixed, in classic client-centred theory the term is used in two principal ways. First, there is the emerging or developing self, which was thus defined by Rogers (1959: 200):

> The organized, consistent conceptual gestalt composed of conceptions of the characteristics of the 'I' or 'me' and the perceptions of the characteristics of the 'I' or 'me' to others and to various aspects of life, together with the values attached to these perceptions. It is a gestalt which is available to awareness though not necessarily in awareness. It is a fluid and changing gestalt, a process, but at any given moment it is a specific entity ...

In a way, this 'self', the experiencing self, is what is differentiated from the organism (as a total openness to experiencing more like that of an infant) through interaction with the environment and, especially, significant others. In the vernacular of Western society, this conceptualisation of the self may be equated with the individual.

Second, there is the self-concept which, in the simplest terms, is the view one has of one's self. But this is intrinsically linked with the way one sees the world (for example, 'homosexuality is wrong' will affect the way one relates to others as well as oneself), so in this book we use the term 'self-structure' to incorporate our values and beliefs about the world in general as well as those about ourselves as individuals (Tolan, 2002: 144–9).

The person for whom there is a notable disparity between their organismic experiencing and self-structure will tend to anxiety, at least a degree of emotional distress and a rigidity of belief and behaviour. The fundamental purpose of person-centred therapy is to facilitate the integration between the organism and the self-structure; and the area of personality where experiences are fully in awareness is termed 'congruence'.

The Acquisition of Conditions of Worth

Individuals have a need for positive regard – in particular from 'significant others' – that is, important people in the immediate environment such as parents and other principal carers. As the self develops, there is also a need for positive self-regard that allows individuals to trust their own perceptions and evaluations of the world as they experience it. In terms of person-centred theory, this position is termed 'having an internal locus of evaluation'. However, the need for positive regard from others, especially those to whom the individual looks for care, protection and nurture, is so strong that this internal evaluation of experience can be easily overwhelmed if love and acceptance is withheld or threatened to be withheld – that is, if they become 'conditional'. So, in order to gain and maintain the positive regard of others, the individual disregards or inhibits the expression of aspects of inner experiencing that conflicts (or seems to conflict) with the needs and opinions of others because to do otherwise would risk the withdrawal of love and acceptance. When this happens, individuals rely on the evaluations of others for their feelings of acceptance and self-regard. They develop an 'external locus of evaluation', distrusting inner experiencing even to the point of abandoning it altogether.

In this way, individuals learn that they are only acceptable, loveable and prized, that is, 'worthy', as long as they conform to the demands, expectations and positive evaluations of others. In this way 'conditions of worth' are acquired. Moreover, they often become so embedded in the self-structure that they are not recognised as originating from outside the individual. So, for example, a person may believe as truth that it is wrong to get angry or that a particular group of people is inferior without having any idea that these are rooted in conditions of worth. In order to maintain a feeling of being valued and accepted, individuals seek or avoid experiences according to how well they fit in with their conditions of worth. Experiences that match these conditions of worth (and therefore the self-structure) are perceived accurately and

accepted; ones that do not are perceived as threatening and are distorted or denied ('distortion' and 'denial' are the two 'defence mecha-
nisms' described in classic person-centred theory – see Rogers, 1959:
227). This leads to 'incongruence' between the self and experience and
in behaviour. It is the process of defence that leads to some expressions
of emotional or psychological distress. Rogers (1959: 228) lists these as
including:

> not only the behaviors customarily regarded as neurotic – rationalization, compen-
> sation, fantasy, projection, compulsions, phobias and the like – but also some of
> the behaviors customarily regarded as psychotic, notably paranoid behaviors and
> perhaps catatonic states.

However, sometimes the process of defence is unable to operate successfully. This can lead to a state of disorganisation (see Rogers, 1959: 229). It
is postulated that this may lead to acute psychotic breakdown. Thus
incongruence arising originally from conditions of worth can be seen as
the root of emotional and psychological distress. The client's incongruence, leading to feelings of vulnerability or anxiety, is the second of
Rogers' (1959: 213) 'necessary and sufficient conditions' for constructive
personality change.

The Six Necessary and Sufficient Conditions for Therapeutic Change

One of the most widespread misassumptions about person-centred theory
is that there are three 'core conditions' (usually named as 'empathy', 'congruence' and 'acceptance' or 'unconditional positive regard'), the practice
of which defines person-centred therapy. This is not so. The famous
hypothesis of the necessary and sufficient conditions for therapeutic change
comprises six statements. From Rogers (1957: 96) these conditions are:

1 Two persons are in psychological contact.
2 The first, whom we shall term the client, is in a state of incongruence, being
   vulnerable or anxious.
3 The second person, whom we shall term the therapist, is congruent or integrated in the relationship.
4 The therapist experiences unconditional positive regard for the client.
5 The therapist experiences an empathic understanding of the client's internal
   frame of reference and endeavours to communicate this experience to the client.
6 The communication to the client of the therapist's empathic understanding and
   unconditional positive regard is to a minimal degree achieved.

Rogers states that, if these conditions are present, positive change will
occur regardless of the orientation of the practitioner. It is important to

note that the hypothesis depends on all six conditions, not merely the so-called core conditions. Exclude any and the proposition falls. Rogers (1957: 100) states this quite unambiguously: 'if one or more of [the six conditions] is not present, constructive personality change will not occur'. Many writers since Rogers have explored this hypothesis from all angles. For example, the title of Bozarth's (1998) paper 'Not necessarily necessary but always sufficient' is self-explanatory.

The assumption that there are 'core' conditions has led people to act, write and think as if it is only these that matter or at least that the 'core' conditions are in some way more important than the other three. Actually, no ranking of the conditions is stated or implied in the original hypothesis or elsewhere in Rogers' writings, although others have attempted to isolate one or another as more 'curative' (examples may be found in the **Further Reading** section below). However, Rogers (1957: 100) does offer a further hypothesis to the effect that: 'If all six conditions are present, then the greater the degree to which Conditions 2 to 6 exist, the more marked will be the constructive personality change in the client.' This still means that it is only collectively and in combination that the conditions are necessary and sufficient. Also, there is no stated or implied ranking of the conditions. Because they are only effective in combination, it is probably a mistake to favour any one above another (see Wilkins, 2010: 43–5).

Symbolisation in Awareness

The importance of the six conditions lies in creating an absence of threat. If the discrepancy between the way that the person sees himself and the world and the evidence of his senses becomes too great, the self-structure will be threatened and its response under threat is to become more rigid. In the therapeutic environment, the practitioner communicates her understanding and acceptance of the client's world in order to provide safety and support. In such an environment, says the theory, the actualising tendency moves the client towards being able to accept more of his organismic experiencing into awareness. This happens naturally and – paradoxically – if the practitioner tries too hard to make it happen, the self-structure is liable to feel threatened and become rigid again.

We use the term *accurate symbolisation in awareness* when the person knows fully what is happening in himself and in the world around him. Distortion and denial of experience involve keeping significant experiences out of awareness or symbolising them inaccurately – that is, the images and narrative do not fit the actual experience of the person. Jane Power talks of abused children who have been taught to suppress the horror of their experiences, and Allan Turner tells of the person whose view of the world is shaken by a life-threatening event. There are many examples in this book of clients moving away from the denials and distortions that give rise to distress towards accurate symbolisation in awareness.

The Non-Directive Attitude

To some extent, non-directivity is the sacred cow of classical client-centred therapy. It is taken as a given that it is a mistake for a person-centred therapist to bring in anything from their own frame of reference. While we agree with this as a general concept, we see that, in dealing with specific presenting problems, knowledgeable practitioners may experience a tension between the therapeutic ideal and what they have to offer their clients. If the therapist has knowledge that may be of benefit to the client but that the client is unlikely to discover themselves, is it really directive to offer it?

You may recognise this tension in some of the chapters in this book (for example, Allan Turner writes about the usefulness of 'critical incident responding' and Barbara Douglas about how helpful keeping a food diary can be to someone experiencing problems with food). At least to some extent this tension is resolved when it is appreciated that what is important is the non-directive *attitude*. An attitude is an approach, an outlook, a manner, not a prescriptive code of behaviour. With respect to being directive it is not so much what the therapist does that is important as what the client experiences. Mearns and Thorne (2000: 191) suggest that: 'The question which should be asked is not "is the therapist behaving directively?" but "is the client being directed?".' So, when introducing something to the therapeutic process of which the client may not be aware, the necessary attitude is to seek to usefully inform it but never to dictate or direct it. Sanders (2006: 82) takes the view that, in experienced person-centred therapists, the non-directive attitude is an aspect of behaviour. They have a way of doing things based on a trust of the client and this, in terms of process, assiduously avoids imposing their will on their clients. Implicitly and sometimes explicitly, the authors of the chapters in this book demonstrate how they do this. However, Wilkins (2003: 89) points out that 'to accurately gauge the client's locus of evaluation is a delicate and complex task'. Given this and also that it is implicit in Sanders' statement (above) that less-experienced therapists may not have fully assimilated a non-directive attitude into their behaviour, our advice is to be cautious and tentative when introducing into a therapy session something from your own frame of reference, however helpful you think it might be. We go further: when in doubt stick to the basic therapist-provided conditions. Also, we strongly suggest that it is wisest and safest to employ new strategies only with expert guidance in the form of further training and/or work with an experienced supervisor.

For those of you wishing to explore the issue of directivity/non-directivity more fully there is a chapter devoted to it in Wilkins (2003: 85–98).

Guide to Further Reading

Reminding Yourself of Basic Person-Centred Theory and Practice

The books listed below represent a few of the many that address the theory and practice of person-centred therapy. They will serve to remind you of the basic premises of these theories and practices.

Mearns, D. and Thorne, B. (2007) *Person-Centred Counselling in Action*, 3rd edn. London: Sage.

A revised and updated version of a classic text.

Sanders, P. (2006) *The Person-Centred Counselling Primer*. Ross-on-Wye: PCCS Books.

This is a little gem of a book that encapsulates the essentials of person-centred theory concisely and in an accessible way. A 'must' for any practitioner or student of the approach.

Tolan, J. (2003) *Skills in Person-Centred Counselling and Psychotherapy*. London: Sage.

From the back cover, the book: 'describes all aspects of the therapeutic relationship ... and demonstrates how the skills and attitudes of the person-centred practitioner are used effectively in a range of counsellor–client interactions'.

Wilkins, P. (2010) *Person-Centred Therapy: 100 Key Points*. London: Routledge.

From the back cover: 'This book offers a comprehensive overview and presents the core theories, advances and practices of the approach in a concise, accessible form.'

Understanding Advances in Person-Centred Theory, Practice and Applications

Of the many books discussing developments in the practice of person-centred therapy and its applications, those listed below are among the best of recent contributions. It is in these that you will find more about the presenting issues examined in this book.

Bozarth, J.D. and Wilkins, P. (eds) (2001) *Unconditional Positive Regard. Rogers' Therapeutic Conditions: Evolution, Theory and Practice*, Vol. 3. Ross-on-Wye: PCCS Books.

Haugh, S. and Merry, T. (eds) (2001) *Empathy. Rogers' Therapeutic Conditions: Evolution, Theory and Practice*, Vol. 2. Ross-on-Wye: PCCS Books.
Wyatt, G. (ed.) (2001) *Congruence. Rogers' Therapeutic Conditions: Evolution, Theory and Practice*, Vol. 1. Ross-on-Wye: PCCS Books.
Wyatt, G. and Sanders, P. (eds) (2002) *Contact and Perception. Rogers' Therapeutic Conditions: Evolution, Theory and Practice*, Vol. 4. Ross-on-Wye: PCCS Books.

This series presents historical accounts, reconsiderations of and research evidence for the efficacy of Rogers' necessary and sufficient conditions. Contributors include doyens of the approach and contemporary theorists and practitioners from across the world.

Cooper, M., O'Hara, M., Schmid, P.F. and Wyatt, G. (eds) (2007) *The Handbook of Person-Centred Psychotherapy and Counselling*. Basingstoke: Palgrave Macmillan.

This book encapsulates the 'state of the art' of person-centred theory and practice. It is a key resource to which over thirty eminent theorists and practitioners from across the world have contributed. It deals with the foundations of person-centred theory, therapeutic practice, settings and client groups and professional issues.

Joseph, S. and Worsley, R. (eds) (2005) *Person-Centred Psychopathology: A Positive Psychology of Mental Health*. Ross-on-Wye: PCCS Books.

In this book, an international collection of writers examine the relationship between the person-centred approach and 'psychopathology'.

Mearns, D. and Cooper, M. (2005) *Working at Relational Depth in Counselling and Psychotherapy*. London: Sage.

Focusing on a relational approach, this book explores how a therapist can enhance their practice.

Sommerbeck, L. (2003) *The Client-Centred Therapist in Psychiatric Contexts: A Therapist's Guide to the Psychiatric Landscape and its Inhabitants*. Ross-on-Wye: PCCS Books.

Highlights ethical and philosophical tensions and possibilities for person-centred practitioners working in psychiatric and other contexts.

Wilkins, P. (2003) *Person-Centred Therapy in Focus*. London: Sage.

In this book, criticisms of the person-centred approach are examined and rebutted. Each chapter sets out these criticisms concisely and then counters them with arguments from a person-centred perspective.

Worsley, R. and Joseph, S. (eds) (2007) *Person-Centred Practice: Case Studies in Positive Psychology*. Ross-on-Wye: PCCS Books.

This is a follow-up volume to Joseph and Worsley (eds) (2005). It comprises accounts of the practice of internationally renowned practitioners and scholars of the person-centred approach.

References

Bozarth, J.D. (1998) 'Not necessarily necessary but always sufficient', in J.D. Bozarth, *Person-Centered Therapy: A Revolutionary Paradigm.* Ross-on-Wye: PCCS Books, pp. 35–42.

Mearns, D. and Thorne, B. (eds) (2000) *Person-Centred Therapy Today: New Frontiers in Theory and Practice.* London: Sage.

Rogers, C.R. (1951) *Client-Centered Therapy: Its Current Practice, Implications and Theory.* Boston, MA: Houghton-Mifflin.

Rogers, C.R. (1957) 'The necessary and sufficient conditions of therapeutic personality change', *Journal of Consulting Psychology*, 21: 95–103.

Rogers, C.R. (1959) 'A theory of therapy, personality, and interpersonal relationships, as developed in the client-centered framework', in S. Koch (ed.), *Psychology: A Study of a Science*, Vol. 3. *Formulations of the Person and the Social Context.* New York: McGraw-Hill, pp. 184–256.

Rogers, C.R. (1967) *On Becoming a Person: A Therapist's View of Psychotherapy.* London: Constable.

Sanders, P. (2006) *The Person-Centred Primer.* Ross-on-Wye: PCCS Books.

Tolan, J. (2002) 'The fallacy of the "real" self', in J. Watson, R. Goldman and M. Warner (eds), *Client-Centred and Experiential Psychotherapy in the 21st Century.* Ross-on-Wye: PCCS Books, pp. 144–9.

Tudor, K. and Merry, T. (2002) *Dictionary of Person-Centred Psychology.* London: Whurr.

Wilkins, P. (2003) *Person-Centred Therapy in Focus.* London: Sage.

Wilkins, P. (2010) *Person-Centred Therapy: 100 Key Points.* London: Routledge.

PART ONE

Life Events

2

A PERSON-CENTRED APPROACH TO LOSS AND BEREAVEMENT

SHEILA HAUGH

It seems somewhat contradictory to propose a person-centred approach to loss and bereavement, given that person-centred therapy is a phenomenological and heuristic attitude to the therapeutic relationship. That is, as person-centred therapists, we are interested in a person's experiencing in the world (the phenomenological stance) and wish to facilitate their discovery of that experiencing (the heuristic stance). From this point of view, the experience of loss may be stated as *the feelings, thoughts and physical sensations associated with any change, actual or perceived, in a person's phenomenological world*. A person-centred approach to working with someone facing loss and bereavement can therefore be stated in the following manner: a commitment to understanding and accepting an individual's experiencing (affective, cognitive and physical) of their losses and to entering their world as fully as is possible. This stance is the same as when working with any experience that the client brings. At the same time, a person-centred approach to loss and bereavement needs to find a way to explain why grief affects us in the way that it does and needs to explain why person-centred therapy is effective for those experiencing loss.

The importance of theory is fourfold. First, theory influences how we see the world and, therefore, our way of being. A theory is simply a suggested explanation for the different phenomena that surround us. We could call theories 'working models' and, of course, the explanations we usually find most plausible are those that also reflect our values and beliefs. I have a belief in the actualising tendency. I see evidence for the actualising tendency all around me and, in consequence, I act as though the actualising tendency is a concrete fact rather than a hypothesis. Belief or disbelief will profoundly affect how I view others in the world (their motives, their trustworthiness) and therefore my way of being in relationships. This is also true of a topic such as loss and bereavement. The values and beliefs I bring to the therapeutic encounter will influence the therapeutic relationship.

Second, if held lightly, theory can help me 'stay in the room' with a client. By this I mean that by having some understanding of what may be happening for a client, I am able to stay centred in myself. Speaking more technically, I am able to remain congruent with myself and therefore more likely to be experiencing unconditional positive regard and expressing that experiencing through empathic responses. It is imperative that theory is 'held lightly'. Rather than pigeonholing a client, my theory should help me stay beside the client. Theory is a general statement about people rather than statements about a particular individual.

Third, clients have often asked me whether or not what they are feeling 'is normal'. Usually, I have only needed to reply with an empathic response. At other times such a reply would have been clearly (on my part) an avoidance and, in that particular moment, an incongruent response. It is obvious that what I believe and understand about reactions to loss and bereavement will influence my response, as I will have some feelings on what is 'normal' grieving. But what if my understanding of loss and bereavement is rooted in a more psychodynamic approach than a humanistic approach and what if I don't even know that there is a difference? If I have not explored the different understandings (theories) of a 'normal' grieving process, I could do my client a great disservice and possibly harm.

Finally, in many ways, loss is the motif that explicitly and implicitly underpins much of our work as therapists. The most explicit content is when someone comes to us because they are bereaved, a relationship is breaking up, they have lost their job, they have moved home or children have left home. I am sure that you can add many more situations. Less obvious issues of loss are present when a client approaches us because they are feeling sad (loss of happiness?), they don't know what to do with their lives (loss of purpose?), life has no meaning (loss of dreams?) or they just don't feel right (loss of ease?). Loss is one of the motifs of life and we should not be surprised that it is a motif of the therapeutic relationship. For these reasons an understanding of loss and bereavement is important in our work as therapists. This chapter is an exploration of such a theory.

Current approaches to loss and bereavement can be described as 'stage' or 'phase' theories. That is, they describe the various points of experience that the bereaved person will go through psychologically. Taking an overview, they usually describe feelings such as numbness, denial, yearning, anger, depression and acceptance. Additionally, they suggest that the 'business' of grief and mourning is to find a way of letting go of the lost object or person in order to be able to move on with existing relationships, to move forward toward new relationships and generally to re-engage with life. In the UK the most well-known and influential of these theorists have been Colin Murray Parkes, William Worden and Elizabeth Kübler-Ross. All three practitioners based their ideas on their work and research with either those experiencing loss or those facing death. Their achievements in this field are worthy of respect for both their expertise and for the reason that they brought to the fore an aspect of human experience that had previously received little attention. Additionally, these stage theories are useful insofar as they have helped to 'normalise' different reactions to grief in a way that has helped me and others, as therapists, to 'stay in the room'. When I have felt lost or overwhelmed by the process I am witnessing when being with a bereaved person, they have helped me to remain accepting of that person's experiencing and thus deepened my empathic understanding of their situation.

Notwithstanding the support that these stage theories have given to those working with the bereaved (and the bereaved themselves), there are a couple of problems with these approaches to grief. First, a general difficulty arises in the way that these concepts have been interpreted. Parkes (1996: xiii), Worden (1991[2000]: 19) and Kübler-Ross (1973[1987]: Preface) have written explicitly that their theories should be seen as a broad picture of reactions to loss. Further, they have also written that their observations of certain stages should not be interpreted as being statements of fixed phases that the bereaved person must be helped to pass through. They are not static stages that are moved along – one to two, two to three, three to four. Rather, loss should be seen as a process that flows backwards and forwards – for example, two to one, one to three, four to two. It is a process that stops, a process that starts, and should be seen as having a flowing dynamic.

Nevertheless, it is clear that often practitioners do expect their clients to go through these stages and, more worryingly, it is their job to help them through that process.

The Dangers of Theory ...

George's wife had, with no prior warning, committed suicide. Although in many ways devastated by this event, George felt no anger towards her. This was a situation that George's counsellor, Jane, found almost impossible to believe and, in consequence, was having difficulty with her acceptance (and consequently her empathy) of his experiencing. Her stance was that 'everybody will feel anger in this sort of situation'. In supervision she came to the realisation that not only was she feeling angry at George's wife, she also expected that a 'healthy' loss response from George would include anger based on her experience and the theories that she knew.

Because Jane misunderstood the descriptive (rather than prescriptive) nature of the theories, a consequence was that her empathy was blocked.

A second aspect of theories of loss and bereavement is that like all theory, they are culturally embedded. Thus we need to note that the context of the stage theories of loss and bereavement is predominantly white and almost exclusively Western. Emotional expression and the understanding made of that expression are culturally defined. For example, in studies made on this subject it was found that Japanese widows and British widows reacted quite differently to the death of their husbands, at least in behaviour, which is different again to the response to bereavement amongst the Hopi of Arizona (Stroebe et al., 1996: 35). To complicate matters further, it is clear that even within a particular culture, for example white European, reactions to loss and bereavement can be quite different. The point is that we need to be extremely circumspect in accepting any theory of grief and grief reactions as being universal. This is not idle relativism: today's theory becomes tomorrow's practice.

A third difficulty, one more specific for person-centred practitioners, lies at a deeper level: that most theories of the bereavement process are rooted in the psychodynamic tradition. In this scheme of thought, the human being has a finite amount of psychic, or emotional, energy that can be distributed into relationships (both internal and external). When a person experiences a loss, the energy attached to that relationship (be it a person or an object) needs to be withdrawn in order for there to be enough energy for a new relationship. From this position it is logical that the task of mourning, or 'grief work' as it is sometimes known, is a process aimed towards letting go of the lost object or person. We need to let go of the lost object or person (withdraw the energy) in order to be able to reinvest (use the energy) in other relationships; in essence we need to break the bond with the loved person. If we did not do this, given that there is only a finite amount of energy, we would eventually run out of psychic energy for any other relationships.

This hypothesis is breathtaking in its hold on everyday thinking and in the wisdom of psychotherapeutic practice. How many times have you heard someone comment about a bereaved person that they seem to be 'getting over it'? Or perhaps you have heard the opposite – 'they don't seem to be getting over it'.

'Not Getting Over It'

Alice spent many months in counselling struggling with 'trying to let go and get over' a finished relationship. A shift occurred when she suddenly realised that she didn't have to 'let go'. In other words, she realised that not only did she not have to break the bond, but she also identified that she didn't need or want to break the bond. Rather, the relationship would be different and, in her words, 'never-ending'. This was irrespective of whether or not she would see her ex-partner again. From that point on, Alice was able to grieve for what she had lost, rather than fight against herself in order to let go of the relationship. Instead, she found a way to integrate the relationship and its ending into her present experiencing of the world.

The therapist realised that she had been anticipating that Alice needed to 'move on' with her life. She had expected Alice would have to leave the relationship behind before she would be able to re-engage with life around her. She was also surprised when Alice identified that her healthy reaction was not to let go of the relationship but simply to accept that it was now different.

The crucial point for person-centred practitioners is that Alice had been caught up in the breaking bonds hypothesis (Stroebe et al., 1996) – as, more importantly, had her counsellor – and it was very difficult to see an alternative, so implicit and deeply imbedded were these ideas of breaking the bond.

A Person-Centred Approach to Loss and Bereavement

The person-centred approach is an organismic approach and takes the position that human beings are open, ever-changing and developing systems. This system includes the past, the present and the future. Human beings are fluid creatures moving in many directions. We are multifarious creatures, forever becoming more of who we might be. Person-centred therapy is based on the connection, the communication and the relationship between two people and a trust in that process. What is the way of describing the dynamics of loss and bereavement in a manner that is more organismic and open, a manner that is more compatible to the person-centred approach and more closely describes our work as we experience it?

Sometimes it is worth stating the obvious. Loss hurts. In a perfect world, with a perfect theory and a perfect therapist, loss will still hurt. It may hurt hardly at all, or it may feel intolerable, but, quite simply, it hurts. What we are attempting to understand is some of 'why' it hurts. Knowing what is happening to my skin, veins and bones when I get a bad cut to the arm will not stop the hurt; neither will understanding loss and bereavement stop the hurt. But just as having some understanding of the way that skin, veins and bones interact may help the surgeon to work in a way that is more healing, so too might having some understanding of the processes of loss help me to be more accepting and empathic with the people I work with.

So what we are really asking is why do different people, at different times, have different reactions to loss and bereavement? There are two areas of person-centred theory that begin to give some answers to these questions. They are the notions of the self-structure and of configurations of self.

Self-Structure

Each person's self-structure is unique to them, an outcome of their life experiences (including their cultural background/context) and a result of the levels of unconditional positive regard that they have received during their life – particularly, though not exclusively, in their early life. It is because of the conditional positive regard we receive that we develop conditions of worth and this means that we learn, at a non-conscious level, which parts of our experiencing are acceptable to others and which are not. As one of the overriding needs of human beings is the need for positive regard, we deny or distort our awareness of those aspects of our experiencing that do not gain positive regard – thus developing a condition of worth. It runs something like, 'I will be loved if ...' or 'I will not be loved if ...'. This is not a thought-out, rational process. It is a process that we are unaware of and one that protects us from the intolerable idea that there are parts of us that are unacceptable to others. Additionally, these parts that are felt as unacceptable to others can often become unacceptable to us.

In Rogers' theory it is inevitable that we will develop conditions of worth. These conditions mean that we have developed incongruence between our organismic valuing system (in this context the psychological aspect of the actualising tendency) and our self-structure. An example may be useful here. In my, white, northern English culture, it could be said as a very general statement that a clear message was 'boys don't cry' (I suspect that this is true of many white English cultures but I prefer not to make that assumption).

A Different Reaction to Loss

Andrew and his sister had been very close as children, spending many hours playing on the farmland that surrounded their childhood home. Despite separations in their teenage years they remained close into their early twenties, Andrew supporting her through periods of mental health problems. In their late twenties and their thirties there was little contact between them, but they re-established their relationship on the birth of his sister's first child. Not long after, Andrew's sister was diagnosed with cancer and died five years later. Throughout the time of her illness, Andrew was her main support and their previous closeness was rekindled. He was knocked for six when she died, grieving both for the loss of her in the present time, and the time that he felt that had been wasted when they had less contact in their youth. His grief took the form of physical symptoms – sleeplessness, aches and pains, lack of appetite.

When faced with this bereavement Andrew had no tears to shed, even though he was feeling distraught and distressed. There are two theoretical possibilities here. First, that although Andrew felt deeply affected by his loss, his lack of tears was his self-concept in congruence with his organismic experiencing. That is, he did not have a condition of worth which told him that boys don't cry, and his not crying was a psychologically healthy response for him as his organismic valuing did not have tears as an expression. On the other hand, if he did have the condition of worth that boys don't cry, although his organismic experiencing may have included expression through tears, his self-concept would have denied or distorted this expression to awareness. He may just feel sick (distortion) or have not felt tearful at all (denial). This makes the point that the same behaviour in different individuals cannot be taken to mean the same levels of congruence between their organismic valuing system and their self-concept.

So here we have one reason why different people react in different ways. In part it will depend on the individual's self-concept. Quite simply, and maybe quite obviously, our different life experiences will have affected the development of our self-concept, the 'who we are', even if our self-concept is totally congruent with our organismic valuing system. This is an important point in relation to cultural differences and bereavement. We should not make the assumption that the healthy grief reaction known to us through our cultural lens – whatever that lens may be – will be equally healthy for those from cultures other than our own. Or, to put it another way, our reactions to bereavement are culturally embedded, and healthy grief reactions vary substantially across cultures. In part, differing grief reactions will also depend on the unique conditions of worth each individual acquires. If I learned that I would gain more unconditional positive regard for being sad and melancholy rather than happy-go-lucky, it may be very difficult for me to risk feeling that the intensity of the loss is receding.

'I Will be Loved if ...'

Joan started to feel guilty that she was having fun sometimes six months after her sister died. One of the aspects of this guilt turned out to be her fear that 'people will think less of me for being happy'. She linked this to the fact that in her early home life it had been frowned on to have 'too much fun – it tempted fate'. In her family of origin she had received more positive regard for being morose than for being happy.

In these discussions of the grieving process and individual reactions in bereavement, we need to be extremely careful of the use of the word 'healthy'. From a person-centred perspective, a healthy grieving process means that any manner in which a person reacts is the healthiest way for them to be right now. We do not know what parts of their self-concept are being protected by their current way of being. We need to trust in their actualising tendency and take a view that they know better than an outsider (for example, the therapist) what is best for them in the moment. This is one reason why I am not able to advocate the idea of directing a client toward their loss issues. I cannot know what a person's conditions of worth may be, and consequently I cannot know how their way of being may be keeping them safe from psychological fragmentation.

Configurations of Self

Dave Mearns and Brian Thorne (2000: 102) describe a configuration as a:

> hypothetical construct denoting a coherent pattern of feelings, thoughts and pre-ferred behavioural responses symbolised or pre-symbolised by the person as reflective of a dimension of existence within the Self.

They are attempting to describe, in theoretical terms, the way in which people experience different parts within themselves. It is hypothetical because we need to remember that these 'parts' of Self cannot be directly observed as entities – they can only be *inferred* from the description given by the person (ibid.: 103). Mearns and Thorne are proposing that these different parts have their own way of experiencing the world, of seeing the world and of behaving in the world – each part having its own self-concept and conditions of worth. This is not a case of dissociative process, rather it is a very usual dimension 'of personality integration' (ibid.: 108). They are clear that a person is aware of these parts or that the part is coming into awareness.

A Cynical Part of Self ...

Angela was experiencing very bad dreams over a Caesarean birth that she had fifteen years previously. The need for a Caesarean, and the loss of the experience of, for her, a natural birth, had been very difficult to accept, particularly as she had been fit and healthy. People had expected her to look on the bright side – she had a healthy baby after all – and she sometimes thought that it would have been easier if someone had died as people would 'expect you to be sad'. Angela had always felt sad about the Caesarean, but the ending of a romantic relationship seemed to have precipitated these bad dreams. Angela also had an internal critic, Mrs Cynic, someone who was very much in awareness for her (that is, it was symbolised in awareness). She would sometimes speak of Mrs Cynic being present at a session. 'Mrs Cynic thinks that I'm making mountains out of molehills – life isn't actually that bad.'

It was clear that one of Mrs Cynic's conditions of worth included the need to be strong and unemotional. As Angela came to feel and trust the acceptance of the counsellor, this configuration started to lose its power over her. She began to notice that in another part of her thought she was a very hurt and vulnerable person, 'not the crybaby Mrs Cynic thinks that I am'. Through counselling Angela came to accept both parts of her. The part which thought that she was making mountains out of molehills, whilst still present, was no longer in ascendancy. The part that had compassion for herself gained some psychological ground and was able to help her grieve for her lost natural birth. Gradually, over time, she had fewer bad dreams and finally they came only very sporadically.

A Change in Understanding of Self ...

When Sophie's husband died, amongst many of the shocks that she experienced was suddenly being referred to as a widow. Looking ashen and physically shaking, very quietly she said, 'I'm not a widow, I'm a wife.' This was not only a statement of fact for Sophie, but it also described a very exact sense of herself. During counselling it became clear that being a wife had many different meanings for her and that these meanings became increasingly differentiated into a number of different parts, or configurations of self. For Sophie, these configurations included 'the loveable person', 'the cared for', 'the carer', 'the homemaker', 'the little girl', 'the unlovable' and 'the bitter person'. Some configurations were clearly in more conflict than others, for example 'the cared for' and 'the unlovable'.

Becoming a widow had challenged Sophie's sense of self and had, over time in her counselling, brought to awareness her different parts. The configurations existed in such a way as to be creative in the face of her loss, and to perform a self-protecting function. To a greater or lesser extent, when somebody suffers a loss, configurations that have previously been experienced as relatively coherent may become jumbled, the experience being one of disjointedness. For Sophie, the external event of her husband dying upset the relatively internal consistency that she had previously experienced. So here we have another reason why people react differently to loss and bereavement. Not only will it depend on the person's self-concept and conditions of worth, but it will also depend on their unique configurations of self and the relationships between these configurations.

Implications for Practice

How does this person-centred theory of loss and bereavement inform a person-centred approach to therapy when working with people facing loss issues? Quite simply, it means that each person is responded to as though there had never been a theory written about loss; that however the person is feeling and behaving is exactly how they need to feel and behave in order to make the loss a part of their life.

This presents a challenge to all practitioners to be open and accepting of all ways in which a person responds to their loss. It challenges us to hold theory *so* lightly that no client is ever forced into a theoretical box. For although responses to loss can be generalised to some extent, we must never forget that each person is unique, with a unique past, present and future, with unique configurations of self and unique conditions of worth. Fundamental to this stance is the concept of the actualising tendency. If 'a definable climate of facilitative psychological attitudes can be provided' then the bereaved person will find 'vast resources for self-understanding' (Rogers, 1986: 197). The vast resource is the actualising tendency, and the 'definable psychological attitudes' are unconditional regard, empathy and congruence.

The Actualising Tendency

The notion of the actualising tendency informs all person-centred theory, philosophy and practice including a theory of loss and bereavement. In Rogers' theory it is the tendency of all living things to maintain and enhance themselves, and he suggested that the only time that the actualising tendency is not present is when the organism is dead. For human beings the tendency expresses itself in a person as an inclination towards safety (maintenance), growth and psychological health (enhancement). The existence of the actualising tendency means that I can trust a person to discover those aspects of themselves that are causing anguish, and trust their movement towards health. I can trust not only where they may go in their loss process, but also how they are feeling and behaving in this moment. Further, from this perspective, any expression of grief, however 'inappropriate' it might seem to the outsider, is understood as the most healthy reaction for the person in that moment.

Being What is Healthiest ...

Lelia and Joe had a stillborn son several weeks before term. They were both devastated by their loss and found that they were unable to help themselves, never mind each other. Lelia had feelings of guilt while Joe felt both angry and numb at the same time. The two had feelings of emptiness and desolation and were in a 'hellish' place. For a time they were estranged from each other, unable to get close. Whatever either of them did seemed inappropriate for the other and there was a time when they were attacking each other emotionally and psychologically. Lelia came close to attacking Joe physically. The loss of their firstborn was, at the time, intolerable.

When their sense of loss was at its most acute, both Lelia and Joe needed to withdraw into themselves to some extent. Occasionally, from outside of their relationship, it was difficult to understand why they were behaving the way they were with each other. However, accepting the presence of the actualising tendency it became understandable in that they both needed psychological safety that the other was unable to offer.

As time passed they slowly found ways to come together and to begin sharing their grief. This was not an easy process and it was not clear how they might survive – either alone or together. In time, their reactions to the death of their son became less acute, though no less profound. They have been able to find something meaningful in the experience both individually and as a couple.

Unconditional Positive Regard, Empathy and Congruence

Unconditional positive regard means being fully accepting of whatever, and however, the bereaved person is feeling and thinking, irrespective of whether the loss was two days ago or twenty years ago. This includes the possibility that the person may not be feeling or thinking anything in particular in relation to their loss. We can never assume that a person will be feeling one way or another, nor that the way that they are feeling is 'healthy' or 'unhealthy' for them because, as I showed above, we do not know what configurations or parts are being touched by their loss. We can only assume that the way in which they are responding is the best for them in this moment. Empathy, as expressed through empathically following responses, is the most uncontaminated way of expressing unconditional positive regard. If there are any skills to be associated with person-centred therapy (as opposed to attitudes) then it is the skill of expressing, verbally or otherwise, our empathic understanding. Congruence is a precondition for the effectiveness of unconditional positive regard and empathy. For me congruence means that in this relationship, in this moment, I am as aware of my experiencing as I can be and my experiencing is also available to my awareness. This experiencing will include my values and beliefs. Very rarely does congruence mean that I share my thoughts or feelings about the person; if I do share something then it is invariably my experiencing in the moment rather than my thoughts. Congruence requires that I have awareness of my own losses and how they may be impacting on me. It requires that I am not closed to their dynamic within me and so not blocking my empathy.

Non-Directivity

Explicit in this approach to loss and bereavement, as with other areas of person-centred work, is the notion of non-directivity. The person-centred approach is non-directive insofar as my intention is simply to attempt to understand the way in which the client is experiencing the world in any given moment and to check that understanding. Thus, I respond to whatever a person is presenting. If they are expressing extreme distress about their loss I will attend to that expression. Likewise if, in the next moment, they are working out what to have for dinner, I will attend to that exploration. However, non-directivity should not be confused with non-influence. It is impossible not to have influence on another – it is an intrinsic attribute of human beings and the meaning of relationships. At the same time it is possible to have the intention to try not to influence. An expression of this intention includes accepting the grieving person's phenomenological experiencing.

The Conditions in Practice ...

Peter found it impossible to make friends or have romantic relationships, and had been very lonely for most of his life. Intimate relationships were simply 'too dangerous'. In fact, the only regular contact that he had with anyone in his life was with his counsellor.

Peter: I will watch *Friends* because it is about youth. I will not watch *One Foot in the Grave* even though I like the actor. I may be this age but I feel like I'm 29 and I will not look ahead. I have not lost my youth.
Counsellor: Looking ahead just takes you too far from being 29.
Peter: I don't look ahead to anything because that is looking ahead to death.

Peter then spoke of his heart condition and how he would probably die in his sleep. He spoke of taking his heart tablets in the evening to guard against this happening. He then said that he was angry that if he committed himself to exams he was taking and he passed them, 'then what?'. He continued:

Peter: I don't live or have relationships because that too all leads to death and I am terrified of the moment of dying.
Counsellor: Almost as though to live at all, in any way shape or form, just brings you closer to the terror of the moment of dying.

He then described how upset he had been when the King had died. The King had been alive all his life and it made Peter realise that his father could also die.

Peter: I spent forty years not living to try and avoid death. Of course this is crazy because I know intellectually that I have to die one day.
Counsellor: I can't escape death, I know that. But I've spent my whole life being crazy trying to avoid it.
Peter: Yes. And so these bloody exams are just another way of doing it.
Counsellor: Another strategy to keep away from it.
Peter: I've never known a relationship – my fantasy relationships are sexual.
Counsellor: The only relationships I've known have been fantasies of sexual relationships.

Peter:	Yes, I can talk a great deal but up until now I've kept my feelings back. Can I be aggressive, can I cry, can I show hurt – I have held those feelings in check.
Counsellor:	Sort of over there [gesticulating to the corner of the room].
Peter:	Yes: you might reject me – I thought today how long can this job situation go on – I could get a job and be out on my ear within a month. I don't know if I can sustain this effort only to get thrown out in a month.
Counsellor:	Get rejected from a job pretty quickly and maybe get rejected from me.
Peter:	Yes, you may be disgusted, think I'm bad, or at very least a snot.
Counsellor:	I might really have some bad feelings towards you.

The counsellor was able to maintain empathic understanding and communicate this to Peter. This meant that she followed his direction, even if at times it seemed not to have a clear sense of continuity (at least to her). Being fully accepting of Peter meant that she did not have any need to do anything but to make sure that she understood all that he was trying to communicate. Her empathy communicated a deep acceptance (unconditional positive regard) of his way of processing his current feelings and concerns. This ability to stay open (congruence) gave Peter the space and opportunity to take a great risk in his relationship with her when he stated that she might be disgusted with him, think him bad or a snot. She did not try to reassure him in any way at this point, remaining empathic to his fear of her rejecting him and thinking him bad.

The Unfolding Process

It is important to remember that grief is a very natural reaction to changes in a person's life and not something to be pathologised. Rando (1993: 5) has suggested that as many as one in three family bereavements result in what she called a 'morbid outcome or pathological patterns of grief' and that there could be 5 to 6 million new cases of 'complicated' mourning in the USA each year. This is an awful lot of apparently abnormal reactions that suggest that what is considered pathological may in fact be very usual. In practice it is injurious to our clients if we cannot accept that any grief response is legitimate and healthy, even if we cannot immediately see the healthy aspect. At the same time it is also injurious to our clients if we separate the conditions of empathy, congruence, unconditional positive regard and the intention of non-directivity. Along with the other conditions, a person-centred theory to loss and bereavement forms a gestalt of responsiveness founded on the maxim 'the client knows best'.

Guide to Further Reading

Bowbly, J. (1998) *Attachment and Loss: Loss, Sadness and Depression*. London: Pimlico.

Kübler-Ross, E. (1973) *On Death and Dying*. London: Tavistock Publications.

Parkes, C.M. (1996) *Bereavement: Studies of Grief in Adult Life*, 3rd edn. London: Penguin Books.

Worden, J.W. (1991[2000]) *Grief Counselling and Grief Therapy: A Handbook for the Mental Health Practitioner*, 2nd edn. London: Routledge.

These four books probably form the basis of much 'practice wisdom' in counselling and psychotherapy in the UK today in relation to loss and bereavement. They are interesting for their delineation of the phases/stages of grief and the tasks of mourning. As noted above, their observations are often taken as prescriptive rather than the stated intention to be descriptive. Nevertheless, the reader is encouraged to bear in mind the philosophical underpinnings of the books, in particular Bowbly, Parkes and Worden, and hold the theories very 'lightly'.

Klass, D., Silverman P.R. and Nickman, S.L. (eds) (1996) *Continuing Bonds: New Understandings of Grief*. London: Taylor & Francis.

This book challenges (then) established ideas on loss and bereavement. In essence they question the idea that grief can be resolved, as that term is commonly understood. As the title implies, they suggest that relationships with the deceased continue in some form and that this relationship is not pathological grieving.

McLaren, J. (1998) 'A new understanding of grief: A counsellor's perspective, *Mortality*, 3 (13): 275–90.

A seminal paper, arguing that offering the conditions of empathy, congruence and unconditional positive regard and following the client's agenda facilitate an individual, diverse process. McLaren also argues (in respect of parental grief at losing a child) that continuing the bond with the deceased is the function of the discourse of counselling.

References

Kübler-Ross, E. (1973 [1987]) *On Death and Dying*. London: Tavistock Publications.

Mearns, D. and Thorne, B. (eds) (2000) *Person-Centred Therapy Today: New Frontiers in Theory and Practice*. London: Sage.

Parkes, C.M. (1996) *Bereavement: Studies of Grief in Adult Life*, 3rd edn. London: Penguin Books.

Rando, T.A. (1993) *The Treatment of Complicated Mourning*. Champaign, IL: Research Press.

Rogers, C.R. (1959) 'A theory of therapy, personality, and interpersonal relationships, as developed in the client-centered framework', in S. Koch (ed.), *Psychology: A Study of a Science*, Vol. 3, *Formulations of the Person and the Social Context*. New York: McGraw-Hill, pp. 184–256.

Rogers, C.R. (1986) 'Client-centered therapy', in I.L. Kutash and A. Wolf (eds), *Psychotherapist's Casebook*. San Francisco, CA: Jossey-Bass, pp. 197–208.

Stroebe, M., Gergen, M., Gergen, K. and Stroebe, W. (1996) 'Broken hearts or broken bonds?' in D. Klass, P.R. Silverman and S.L. Nickman (eds), *Continuing Bonds*. Philadelphia, PA: Taylor & Francis, pp. 31–44.

Worden, J.W. (1991[2000]) *Grief Counselling and Grief Therapy: A Handbook for the Mental Health Practitioner*, 2nd edn. London: Routledge.

3

PERSON-CENTRED APPROACHES TO TRAUMA, CRITICAL INCIDENTS AND POST-TRAUMATIC STRESS DISORDER

ALLAN TURNER

Introduction

Although the effects are never the same for one individual as another, most people have a rough idea of what happens to a person who suffers trauma – but what is actually going on inside that person and how can person-centred theory help us make sense of these experiences? There are person-centred explanations for the process and effects of traumatisation and its consequences. Moreover, person-centred therapy is an effective way of working with people experiencing trauma, including post-traumatic stress disorder (PTSD).

A Person-Centred Understanding of Trauma

We all have a self-structure – an organised configuration of perceptions of the self that are admitted into our awareness. Put simply, it is who we think we are, and includes an expectation of how we will react in predictable situations. It also includes an understanding of the environment in which we live. In the normal course of events things happen in life that comfortably fit within our self-structure, or are sufficiently close to it for us to make minor adjustments to it without any difficulty or anxiety. If significant events are far beyond our expectations then we have difficulty in symbolising them in awareness. A traumatic event contains elements that are likely to be so far beyond our previous experience that we initially find it difficult to incorporate the new experience into our self-concept. We and the world are not as we have assumed and we no longer know how to cope. Also, the environment that we thought that we understood and could predict has turned out to be unpredictable. This sets up anxiety – sometimes of an extreme nature. In terms of person-centred theory, anxiety is one of the consequences of incongruence.

By definition, at the beginning of trauma a serious, life-threatening, (or thought to be life-threatening) event takes place. However, as well as a threat to physical existence, trauma often involves a perceived or subceived threat to the self-concept and therefore to everything that the person experiences as 'me'. This is fundamentally subversive and promotes anxiety and fear. Moreover, a traumatic event can be so shocking, and so far beyond the model of the world that the person has constructed (or introjected), that they are unwilling, or unable, to reconstruct their 'self' and 'world model' in order to incorporate the new information. This threatens to change these concepts so fundamentally that, effectively, the former 'self' will cease to exist. Faced with annihilation of the self, it is not surprising that people find the new information difficult to embrace. Even those willing to attempt it undertake an extremely difficult task.

The predominant importance of 'self' also explains why responses to the same traumatic event are so individual. The event itself is not the most important variable; the critical variable is the self-structure of the traumatised person. Obviously the more dreadful the event, the greater the likelihood of a significant variation between the existing self-structure and the new symbolisation necessary in order to reflect accurately the world and self now experienced. Thus trauma goes much further than physical harm and death; it threatens our most basic and personal assumptions about the world and how we understand it.

Rogers' concept of incongruence is especially important in understanding what happens to people who experience a critical incident or are in some other way traumatised. In the case of trauma work it is the gap between the clients' former understanding of their selves and/or the world, and the world that they are now confronted with, that results in incongruence. 'Processing' is the task of accurately symbolising the new information and incorporating it into the new model – of making sense of what has happened. In most cases that gap between the existing self-structure and the traumatising experience is narrow enough to enable the experience to be assimilated into the self-structure fairly readily. (This is not to suggest that the process is painless or easy.) However, in some cases the gap between self-structure and the traumatising experience is currently too great for assimilation. The actualising tendency will continue to prompt the person, through a range of uncomfortable or painful feelings, to pay attention to the experience, and they may not need professional help to do so. Most people's actualising tendency excellently assists them in processing a traumatic event.

Common Reactions to and Experiences of Trauma

The words 'stress' and 'depression' have become so overused that they have ceased to be meaningful. If a client is referred to me with 'stress' or 'depression', I have little idea what to expect. Likewise 'trauma' is slipping into our everyday language and being devalued as a consequence.

Asi

Asi, a young woman, phoned me because her boyfriend, Paul, had left her. After we made the first appointment I asked her why she had chosen me from the many counsellors in the Yellow Pages. Asi said that it was because I was the only one who advertised my experience of working with trauma victims. She felt confident that I could help her because it had been traumatic for her when Paul left her. Whilst this may be the colloquial meaning of trauma for a young person, it was not the meaning that I had intended when placing the advert.

Over the last decade I have worked with hundreds of people who have been involved in 'critical incidents'. A critical incident is one in which someone is killed or there was good reason at the time to think that someone might be killed. The reaction of those witnessing the event is horror. Horrifying events of this nature and those involving threats to life or extreme loss are what I mean by a traumatic event. These events include (for example) bank raids, road, rail and air crashes, natural disasters and terrorist incidents. The severity of people's responses seems to be influenced by:

- The amount of time elapsed since the event.
- The severity of the event.
- The personal meaning of the incident.

People often react in ways that they would not have predicted before the event. Those whose self-concept predicts that they will function well sometimes end up hiding in the toilet or in a cupboard. Conversely, sometimes those who would expect themselves to be paralysed and powerless to take action by such an event are not.

Carmen

A gunman who fired at the ceiling ran from the building when confronted by Carmen, who was angered by his actions. Her self-image was that of the mild, polite, middle-aged woman society expected her to be. In fact, this was a misleading picture – she fiercely protected her branch when she thought it was under attack.

A major part of the response to a traumatic event is caused by its extra-ordinary nature – it is frighteningly outside normal experience. Part of the process of recovery from trauma is to 'normalise' the event. This involves the traumatised person ceasing to see what happened as incomprehensible and realising that their reaction to the episode is the normal reaction of many people faced with a similar occurrence. The key to understanding responses to trauma is grasping the importance of the disjuncture between the normal and the extraordinary. For example, it is the experience of suddenly encountering the extraordinary that accounts for the extremely commonly reported experience of sleep disruption.

John

When John went home on the night of the car accident he couldn't sleep. His mind was racing, but he later found it difficult to say what he was thinking about. Small fragments of the evening leading up to the accident and subsequent rescue by emergency services kept coming into his mind. He was over-aroused and sleep eluded him. On the subsequent nights John was aware of dreaming. He said that the dreams were not really connected to the accident. In one dream, his wife had gone on a routine journey, but didn't come back. Another night he was flying a plane and the controls didn't work properly – 'a bit like the accident?' the counsellor had asked.

About 80 per cent of people involved in a critical incident report difficulty in sleeping afterwards. They have been confronted with a great deal of new information that is beyond the range of their personal experience. They are kept awake by excessive brain activity because their minds have not yet assembled a coherent symbolisation of the event. After a day or so the feeling of a 'racing brain' diminishes and then, usually on the second and subsequent nights, trauma-related dreams may occur. This is a continuation of the process of making order out of chaos, explaining the inexplicable and bringing meaning to the meaningless. Unfettered by the demands and rationale of the waking world, the dreaming mind can explore a wide range of possibilities in its search for meaning and explanation. The actualising tendency is doing its work, prompting the organism to symbolise experience in awareness as accurately as possible.

Dreams following trauma will often explore the event from every conceivable angle, the mind experimenting with different versions of it. Sometimes the ending is much more desirable; in others the incident becomes worse.

Morag

The robbers had entered the bank from the rear, through the manager's office. The staff ran from the front into the street. Morag, an assistant manager on duty at the time, dreamt of being chased through a house that had an endless number of rooms. Her mind had focused on the running aspect of the incident. Some of her colleagues also reported dreams involving running and being chased.

People caught up in critical incidents need to symbolise the incident accurately and give it personal meaning. Immediately following a critical incident, traumatised people often experience difficulty in concentrating. At the root of this is a preoccupation with symbolising the event. The more quickly a person can symbolise the event the quicker this phase passes. A recovering person normally passes through this phase within a week to ten days. If individuals prevent themselves from engaging in the processing, then they risk experiencing difficulties later.

Just as people have a self-concept, so too do they have a 'world concept'. Whereas the 'self-concept' is a symbolisation of who they think they are and how they function, the 'world concept' describes the world – how it works, what one can expect and therefore how the 'self-concept' needs to be to function in the individual's 'world concept'. It is often the case that there is something about a traumatic event that fundamentally threatens the self-concept, world concept or both (self-structure). An intolerable incongruence is created and some people solve that difficulty by denial or avoidance. The incongruence causes their mind to 'blow a fuse' every time they think about it, so the solution that they adopt is not to think about it and thus the normalisation process is frustrated or even stopped. This can result in PTSD (see below).

The new world in which critical incident survivors find themselves in contains much higher levels of danger than they had previously contemplated. We all know that natural disasters, accidents and armed robberies happen, but this knowledge takes on a new meaning when it is *ME*, or *MY* loved ones, who are directly affected. What was an intellectually appreciated distant possibility has become local and personal. The fact that 'nature' or the perpetrators of a crime care so little for the well-being and survival of the person who has experienced a critical incident represents a direct and dangerous threat to their self-structure, in particular their concept of the world. It is also reasonable to conclude that the world contains other unsuspected threats. In this way, the world concept is perceived to be unreliable and thus prediction of dangers is, at best, untrustworthy and probably inaccurate! This is both psychologically and physically threatening. In all cases the linking factor is the realisation that what was assumed to be trustworthy is proved not to be so. To 'fully function' they need to adjust to new circumstances quickly.

Emma

Emma liked her job. In the three years that she had worked at the bank she had developed good friendships and thought of the bank as a safe place where her self-esteem was enhanced. However, since the armed raid, which the police suspected was an 'inside job', she has felt physically unsafe, uncertain about whom to trust and reluctant to go to work.

Post-Traumatic Stress Disorder (PTSD)

Having been involved in a critical incident, some people try to cope by avoiding thinking about it. In terms of person-centred theory, this can be understood as distorting or denying the experience, which means that recovery doesn't happen in a healthy, normal way. In more extreme case, 'avoidance' of psychologically processing the traumatising event and its real meaning may result in post-traumatic stress disorder (PTSD). If an event, such as a sudden death, is way beyond our expectations and control we have difficulty in symbolising it. For some people, admitting such a possibility poses a great threat to their self-structure and they deny or distort their experience rather than accept such fundamentally threatening new knowledge. Many discover that the world is a more dangerous place than they had previously suspected. Rather than tending towards being 'fully functioning', a person traumatised to this degree is rigid and defensive, having difficulty in adapting to new circumstances – so someone experiencing PTSD is an extreme illustration of Rogers' 'maladjusted person'.

Whereas, in terms of person-centred theory, incongruence is usually seen as a consequence of conditions of worth, the important aspect of incongruence in critical incident responding is in relation to inaccurate, or reluctant, symbolisation, not conditions of worth. Colleagues suggest that the 'conditions of worth' argument still applies – it is those who have been previously damaged by external conditions of worth who have greatest difficulty in symbolising the new information but I do not see this correlation in the people with whom I work. It seems to me that it was the train crash or a gunman, and so on, which has caused the disturbance, not a condition of worth. I theorise that those who have experienced empathy, unconditional acceptance and truthful relationships (congruence) will be better able to re-symbolise and so to incorporate the new world revealed by the incident. They are closer to Rogers' concept of the 'fully functioning person'. Their active and less-inhibited self-structure is able to complete the task quickly. Those whose exposure to the 'core' conditions was much more limited find incorporation of the new information much more difficult.

The Effect of Repeated Traumatisation

When working with people who have experienced a critical incident, I always make a point of asking if anything similar has happened to them before. Often for people involved in a second or subsequent incident there is a cumulative effect. This is frequently so when the client was not debriefed after the first incident, or has chosen to deal with the original event by 'putting the incident out of their mind'. This strategy may have worked for a while, even for a number of years, but the new incident resurrects earlier, unresolved problems that now refuse to go away.

Even the idea of asking a question, let alone specific reference to a subject not referred to by the client, may be anathema to some classical person-centred practitioners. I find it acceptable. I am not an expert on any individual client, but I am widely experienced in how people react to, and recover from, critical incidents. I will always wish to ask my questions in a tentative, inquiring way, not from the position of one who interprets the client's experience. Ultimately I hope to help the client 'normalise' their experience.

Amy

Amy was involved in a road accident in which a pedestrian was seriously injured. I saw her a few days afterwards and she insisted that she wanted to put the whole thing behind her and return to work as soon as possible. Amy cancelled the next session. Three weeks later she was involved in a 'shunt' at a roundabout and when I saw her again she had not slept for days and doubted if she would ever return to work. The second, minor incident had breached the defences that she had carefully constructed around processing the first.

With clients who have been involved in many critical incidents, eventually the opposite happens and they seem to become inured to the process.

Rafiq

Bank clerk Rafiq had been in thirty raids. He seemed pretty blasé about the whole thing and I assume that his world model had long since been adjusted to incorporate bank raids, which he seemed to see as an occupational hazard.

The Role of Psychological Processing in Critical Incident Debriefing

In the light of the descriptions and discussion above, the potential benefits of 'psychological processing' start to emerge. Psychological processing is a structured meeting giving the client an opportunity to understand the facts of an event, with particular reference to sensory memories of the incident. In addition, links between cognitive and emotional memories will be made. Also, the client is helped with normalisation by having commonly occurring reactions and responses explained to them. Group sessions are more helpful than individual sessions in the early stages, particularly for a complicated event. A complicated event is one where a single person's eyewitness account of the event is unlikely to explain the event fully because significant aspects of the episode occurred in more than one place.

It is very difficult to symbolise an event accurately if one does not understand its mechanics. The difficulty increases if the meanings of individual components of the event are unclear to those involved.

The Debriefer

The bank was attacked at two points simultaneously – by a ram-raid from behind, and a sledgehammer attack from the front. Staff members ran in different directions, each fleeing the danger as they perceived it. In the confusion at the time and as they relived the incident later on, no one really understood why the others running in the opposite direction had taken the action that they did. It was very difficult for those involved to build up an accurate picture of what had actually happened. This hampered their accurate symbolisation of the event. The first task of the debriefer working with the bank workers was to enable them all to understand the whole process of the raid.

Processing the event is vital. As well as understanding what actually happened, the exact sequence of events – who did what and when – is necessary for those involved to make sense of it. In this process the responder (that is, the person facilitating the psychological processing) pays great attention to constructing a detailed and accurate picture of what happened. A typical bank raid lasts only a minute or so. To debrief such an event, even if there are only a few staff involved, could easily take an hour-and-a-half – with a great deal of time being given to understanding the physical and psychological responses that have already occurred and also to discussing the likely duration of such responses.

In a psychological processing session, the debriefer and client(s) go through the detail from 'safe place to safe place'. This often means starting with the journey to work, what the day had been like prior to the incident, right through to the person being home again. However, a proportionately large amount of the time will be spent processing even the smallest aspects of the central event. In particular the debriefer (the person responsible for the meeting) will be interested in whatever information each sense has recorded – 'What did you see?', 'Could you smell anything?' and 'Did he touch you?' are all typical questions. Bringing such detail into consciousness helps people to understand and process fully the incident. This reduces the risk that experience is held out of awareness because it is too threatening.

Zoe

In the shopping mall, Zoe suddenly became fearful when a man wearing a distinctive T-shirt walked towards her. Then she remembered that she had been told at the Critical Incident Response meeting that this might happen. Her mind had hooked onto a memory from last week when the robber in the DIY store, where she works, was wearing a similar T-shirt. She realised that 'that was then and this is now', that the fear she experienced related to the robbery, not the man walking towards her.

The recovery, which so frequently occurs, is an elegant example of the actualising tendency in action. Usually, the new information about the world and the individual's part in the world is successfully incorporated into the internal models of both the self and world. This process seems to accelerate, become more complete and robust, if a psychological processing meeting is experienced. The debriefer assists the process of symbolising what has happened by offering the conditions of unconditional positive regard, empathy and genuineness. Within such an accepting framework, the individual can be supported in remembering accurately what happened and begin to incorporate the experience into his or her self-structure.

The majority of people recover successfully from critical incidents, but a few do not. There is some correlation between the seriousness of the incident and the time that it takes to recover. Hence those involved in a major air crash are likely to take longer to recover than those who were involved in a car accident 'shunt' at a roundabout. Also more people are likely to be affected by a 'serious' event. For example, if a gun is fired during a bank robbery more people will be adversely affected than if they were merely told by the robber that he had a gun, but they did not see it. Even this knowledge gives us very little guidance to help us understand why some people have more difficulty than others.

Most people process the majority of the symptoms of traumatisation in the first three or four weeks. These symptoms will typically include:

- Tiredness
- Neck and shoulder aches
- Headaches
- Irregular sleep patterns
- More dreaming than is usual for the client
- Hyper-vigilance
- Intrusive and unwanted thoughts
- Flashbacks
- 'What if' thinking (the client is constantly troubled by imagining how his/her actions could have changed the outcome)
- Anxiety
- Feeling vulnerable
- Guilty feelings

If the processing task is not completed soon after the incident, the symptoms could continue longer, sometimes for many years. Therapists involved in trauma counselling, as opposed to those responding to critical incidents, are likely to encounter many of these difficulties when they have been present for months or even years. Typical persistent symptoms, when the client has been unable to symbolise events into awareness, include:

- Intrusive and distressing recollections, including images, thoughts or perceptions – these can occur at almost any time. They are powerful, intrusive memories.
- Dreams – sometimes the dream is recurring, at other times the exact content is different, but the same emotional scene is played out time and time again. A dream stemming from a critical incident is likely to contain components from the original event, rather than be an accurate representation of it.
- Feeling as if the event is recurring, including a sense of reliving the experience, illusions, hallucinations and dissociative flashbacks, including when waking or when drunk. Sometimes the power of this is underestimated. These perceptions can be so vivid that the client cannot perceptually separate them from reality.
- Intense distress if exposed to reminders of the event. The reminders can be almost anything. Photographs, seeing the work uniform, encountering work colleagues, places, sounds.
- 'Re-living' the event if one is exposed to reminders of it. This is similar to the third point listed above, but the event seems to run again and during that time the client is back in the event, not here with the counsellor.

Shaleena

Shaleena became anxious in a glass-sided lift in her office complex when a young colleague deliberately made it shake 'for a laugh'. She had escaped from the Boxing Day tsunami a few months earlier. Suddenly her perception was that she was back on the Indian Ocean island and not at work. She heard the water, saw it rushing towards her and even felt it coming up her legs.

Brian I

Brian had dreamt about his girlfriend, who was his pillion rider in a motorcycle crash in which she was killed, almost every night for twenty-five years.

In the examples above, the task of processing the event has not been completed and the actualising tendency, working insistently, tries to re-present unprocessed material – not allowing the individual to settle for denial and distortion. We know that the people who are most likely to suffer from PTSD are those whose defence against difficulty is 'avoidance' of the prompting of the actualising tendency based in a real fear of re-experiencing the event. Such avoidance is usually very unsuccessful and the likelihood is that normal life will be seriously impaired. Such people tend to present asking for help to make the impairing symptoms go away. (The person who has been able to symbolise and assimilate the event rapidly is not avoiding and will not have such symptoms.) In effect, as therapists, we are being asked to collude in the process of ignoring the prompting of their actualising tendency. Some people can be remarkably persistent in their avoidance.

Bill I

Bill, a truck driver, who was involved in a multiple fatal accident, would proudly say that things were going well, he had managed to put the accident out of his mind. However, he was unable to return to work, drive his car, read a newspaper or watch many television programmes, in case they brought him reminders of the event. It seemed that the event was very much present for him, ready to be re-activated by a range of stimuli.

An image that seems to be helpful to people, is that of the mind containing many rooms and each room contains a memory of an event as if it is still happening. They are in dread of entering the room in which memories of the traumatic event are stored because they fear that the door will close behind them and they will be trapped with that memory forever. My wish for them is that they will be able to enter that room at will and leave with equal ease. I offer to enter the room with the client and stay there with them. When they want to leave I'll exit with them. I never force or trick them into entering the room and, in keeping with the non-directive attitude, I will not detain them there longer than they wish.

Claire

Claire was twenty years old when her brother-in-law hanged himself in the house where she lived. She had guessed that something was wrong when he did not return from the toilet. She took his two young children to a neighbour before forcing the bathroom lock and finding him. For the next two weeks she was the 'strong one', breaking bad news to friends and family, arranging the funeral and taking responsibility for her family, and his. She was referred for counselling by her employers because she was no longer able to attend work and was constantly troubled by intrusive thoughts and hyper-vigilance. Counselling gave Claire an opportunity to 'tell her story' and enter the rooms that she had been avoiding. It took a few sessions and the counsellor was careful to ensure that Claire clearly understood that the work could proceed at her pace.

Processing a Traumatic Event

In processing a traumatic event, the all-important task is for the person to re-symbolise to include the new, and often painful, knowledge that is its consequence. Until they are able to do this they live in a state of incongruence between the world that they want to live in, the self that they see living in that world, and reality. They are trapped between two worlds, one dead, and the other powerless to be born (Arnold, 1865).

Meeta

Meeta, a much-loved adult daughter, was killed by a drunk driver. Ram and Usha, her parents, struggled to come to terms with a world that contains such injustice and one that could suddenly snatch the future from them. They were tortured by 'what ifs' where they constantly imagined scenarios where their daughter survived. They found ways of blaming themselves for 'not getting her up earlier', and so on. As they became increasingly introspective they lost interest in their grandchildren. They became bitter at the leniency of the legal system that sentenced the driver to less than two years in prison.

Krystina

Krystina, a bereaved wife, discovered that her husband, Lech, had a secret life about which she knew nothing. The inescapable conclusion was that she had not been living with the man that she thought she knew and loved. Her task was a massive one. Not only did she have to construct a future world in which her husband was a memory, rather than a living reality, but his secret life meant that she had to reconstruct the meaning of many things that they had done together over the years. Such reconstruction is extremely difficult because it is usually accompanied by the pain of loss as the person grieves for all of their old reality.

Other circumstances may leave the world virtually the way it was but the individual's understanding of self must change.

Brian II

Brian had been involved in a motorcycle accident in which his young girlfriend had been killed, twenty-five years before going to therapy. He blamed himself and ever since he had been unable to come to terms with his part in the accident. Friends and family had misguidedly thought that he would get over it if they didn't keep reminding him of the event. It became the demon that was driven underground and from that place acquired even more power. Brian was tortured by frequent dreams and panic attacks as his actualising tendency prompted him to symbolise the accident, but his conscious mind tried to push it away. He feared that to listen to the prompting of his actualising tendency would mean being trapped in the 'room containing the memory'. For twenty-five years the battle raged between his actualising tendency and his fear of processing the events and thereby accurately symbolising the event. After a few years he discovered various illegal drugs and these would give him temporary relief whilst extracting their own addictive price. My first contact with him was when his wife contacted me in a last-ditch attempt to save her marriage because the drug habit seemed to be building up again and she did not know if she could take any more. In our first session I got an overview of what had happened to Brian from the accident until the present time. In the second, two-hour, session Brian talked in detail about the accident, his emotional mistreatment at the hospital and the 'wall of silence' from his friends and family following the accident. In the next few sessions Brian talked about his drug habits and how he had accidentally discovered drugs as an escape from the dreams. I only saw him for a few sessions and then had a 'follow-up' a few months later to ensure that the apparent changes were being sustained – they were.

Even though we think of person-centred therapy as non-directive, early in our relationship I offer a client what could possibly be seen as a direction. I explain the theory behind my way of working – the incongruence between the two worlds that the client is struggling with. I tell them that, in my opinion, they are most likely to bridge that incongruence if we start by examining the original event closely. I explain that this will involve describing and thinking about as many aspects of the event as possible, that this might be a long process and it is often a painful one. I will encourage them to enter as fully as they can into the process but assure them that I will not push or rush them. In my experience this helps clients to construct the foundations upon which to build an accurate symbolisation of the event. It also helps me to understand the event clearly, which makes it easier and safer for me to accompany the client on their journey.

Ken

Ken referred himself for trauma counselling a few weeks after his second road accident and after being threatened with serious assault by another driver when picking up his grandchildren from school. I explained that I would like him to describe in detail the three incidents to help him 'make sense of them'. He expressed reluctance to do this, saying that he was hoping that I would teach him a way to forget about the incidents. Nevertheless, over the next dozen sessions he chose to talk about the incidents in detail, even after starting each session by telling me that he didn't want to. As he talked I would sometimes ask questions, or invite him to draw diagrams, so that I fully understood the circumstances of each incident. Sometimes I would 'normalise' his subsequent reactions. He saw my work with him as a mystery. It didn't seem that I was doing anything, he would tell me, and yet he found himself overcoming his difficulties.

Cleveland

Cleveland was attacked by a large dog. During the day he knew that dogs could not walk up vertical walls, but his fear was that at night they could! Although he lived on the fourth floor he could not sleep safely with the window open even in hot weather for fear that the dogs could enter. I made no attempt to deny, or correct, his bizarre reality. At the time he tells me about the dogs, I am in his world and in that world dogs can walk up vertical walls at night – viewed from that perspective his terror is sane and rational. I help, not by denying the existence of the world that he inhabits, but by entering it too. If I can't be trusted with such small things, how can I be trusted with the bigger fears?

The client has a genuine choice in deciding how they want to tackle the task. The alternative is for me to be with them in a much less 'event chronological' way as they explore aspects of their experience – probably more akin to that which one would expect from a person-centred therapist not specifically addressing a traumatising event. I will offer the 'therapist conditions' and be with my clients as they explore their worlds in whatever way is right for them. However, when I work with traumatised people most opt to start by talking about the event, realising that the conversation will be difficult if I don't understand what has happened to them. They will almost always say as much, or as little, as they feel safe to say. They know that they will be overwhelmed if they expose too much so it is always safe to trust the client's own judgement in such matters. Just as is the case when working with clients who have been abused, so traumatised clients will carefully check that it will not harm the therapist to hear their stories. Gradually the clients come to trust their own conclusion that I am strong enough to hear their story and only then can it start to emerge in a way that can allow accurate symbolisation of the event and its consequences.

This process has occurred many years after the original event and it has still been successful. Both for the client and for me, this is often very painful. No matter what the event, there will always be a strong element of loss present and it is the genuine acceptance of that loss that engages the pain. Yet it is also this process that is healing. Only when this is achieved can the client fully invest emotional energy elsewhere. It may often mean the exploration of the real meaning of many aspects of a person's life. For some people this will include their religious beliefs and their relationship with God.

Jacqueline

Jacqueline was killed in a road traffic accident ten days before she was going to get married. The funeral took place in the church that had been booked for her wedding and the same guests attended. Her friends and work colleagues told me that they struggled to continue believing in a loving, all-powerful, just God who could at best permit such a thing to happen or, at worst, cause it.

Needless to say, whatever the belief (or non-belief) of the therapist, part of the job when working with people who have lived through a critical incident is to attend to the sometimes agonising struggle that they have with fitting what has happened to them into their belief systems.

Working with trauma, I am struck by Rogers' description of the fully functioning person. In particular, I am struck by the fluidity of being that allows the acceptance of new information, which is then readily incorporated into the person's model of the world and the willingness to take account of new circumstances. This is obviously an idealised position and it would be difficult for any of us to achieve it quickly if we had lost someone close to us. However, I think that it gives a good model of an optimum attitude that will help a person to recover from trauma. For clients who are trapped in their trauma the reverse is true.

Bill II

The twenty-year-old Claire was able to recover from the trauma of discovering her brother-in-law hanged in the bathroom after only a few sessions of counselling. By contrast, truck-driver Bill found his world constantly contracting as he avoided the prompting from his actualising tendency to look at the circumstances surrounding the fatal accident in which he was the sole survivor. In order to avoid reminders he had stopped reading newspapers, watching television news or dramas for fear of reference to fatal road accidents.

To 'recover', traumatised clients must reconstruct their worlds, and by entering their worlds I become a companion in this task. I make no attempt to influence the construction of the new world, but I stand with the client, I bear witness to the new construction. The client is no longer alone in the task.

Guide to Further Reading

Joseph, S. (2004) 'Client-centred therapy, post-traumatic stress disorder and post-traumatic growth: Theoretical perspectives and practical implications', *Psychology and Psychotherapy Theory Research and Practice*, 77 (1) 101–9.

As its title suggests, this is a theoretical consideration of PTSD in the context of the person-centred approach. Stephen Joseph shows that Rogers' account of the threat-related psychological process is largely consistent with contemporary trauma theory.

Joseph, S. (2005) 'Understanding post-traumatic stress from the person-centred perspective', in S. Joseph and R. Worsley (eds), *Person-Centred Psychopathology: A Positive Psychology of Mental Health*. Ross-on-Wye: PCCS Books, pp. 190–201.

Stephen Joseph considers PTSD from a person-centred perspective. Again the emphasis is on PTSD, in contrast to my emphasis, which is from a point just days after the traumatic incident. Joseph's explanation of the underlying psychopathology, from a person-centred perspective, is similar to that which I have proposed. He also proposes a concept of 'post-traumatic growth' as the client recovers from PTSD. Given the title of the book, this is not surprising.

Joseph, S., Williams, R. and Yule, W. (1997) *Understanding Post-Traumatic Stress: A Psychosocial Perspective on PTSD and Treatment*. Chichester: Wiley.

This major work focuses on PTSD, whereas this chapter's focus is on appropriate therapeutic responses and understandings within the first few weeks following a critical incident that may later lead to a diagnosis of PTSD. The minimum diagnostic period for PTSD described by DSM IV is one month if Acute and three months if Chronic (six months for delayed onset.) This book examines PTSD from a variety of theoretical perspectives.

Mearns, D. (2009) *Working with Trauma in a Person-Centred Way.* Available at: www.davemearns.com/Trauma Belfast Oct09.pdf (accessed 28 March 2011).

In this series of Powerpoint slides, Dave Mearns presents his ideas about working with a traumatised person in a person-centred way. He does this with reference to his concept of working at relational depth.

Mearns, D. and Cooper, M. (2005) 'Earning the right to work with Rick: A traumatised client', in D. Mearns and M. Cooper, *Working at Relational Depth in Counselling and Psychotherapy.* London: Sage, pp. 98–112.

This chapter comprises a practical account of working with a traumatised person in the context of relational depth.

References

Arnold, M. (1865) 'Stanzas from the Grande Chartreuse', www.poetryfoundation.org/poem/172861 (accessed 5 July 2011).

Biswas, R. (2003) 'Breaking the silence over India's last taboo', *Panos* (Calcutta), 21 August.

DSM IV (1996) *Diagnostic Criteria from DSM-IV.* Washington, DC: American Psychiatric Association.

Maddi, S.R. (1996) *Personality Theories: A Comparative Analysis*, 6th edn. Toronto: Brooks/Cole Publishing Co.

Pescitelli, D. (1996) *An Analysis of Carl Rogers' Theory of Personality.* Available at: www.wynja.com (accessed 2 February 2011).

Rogers, C.R. (1959) 'A theory of therapy, personality and interpersonal relationships, as developed in the client-centered framework', in S. Koch (ed.), *Psychology: A Study of a Science*, Vol. 3. *Formulations of the Person and the Social Context.* New York: McGraw-Hill, pp. 184–256.

Rogers, C.R. (1961) *On Becoming a Person: A Therapist's View of Psychotherapy.* London: Constable.

Strachey, L. (2007) *Queen Victoria*, Chapter 7 'Widowhood'. Available at: http://womenshistory.about.com, part of The New York Times Company (accessed 2 February 2011).

4

PERSON-CENTRED THERAPY WITH ADULTS SEXUALLY ABUSED AS CHILDREN

JANE POWER

The issue of child sexual abuse has sparked controversy since Freud (1896) presented, and later abandoned, a theory of 'child seduction'. Kinsey's research revealed high percentages of adult–child sexual contact (Kinsey et al., 1953), but was discredited. In the 1970s, feminist organisations 'rediscovered' child sexual abuse, placing it in the context of gender and power relations, and legislation and child protection gradually improved. Evidence from ChildLine, which offers confidential telephone support to children, shows that one in five girls and one in ten boys have experience of sexual abuse (NSPCC, 2007): 95 per cent of the girls and 56 per cent of the boys were abused by males; 5 per cent of the girls and 44 per cent of the boys were abused by females.

Being sexually abused can have a major impact on the development of a child's self, their behaviour and on their psychological adjustment in the world. Given that one in six adult clients coming for counselling may have been sexually abused as children (Cawson et al., 2000), therapists need to become knowledgeable about and aware of this still contentious issue.

Although Rogers put children's relationships with their carers at the heart of his theory, there is almost nothing in the early person-centred literature about childhood sexual abuse. Many person-centred therapists have gained extensive experience from working with adults who were abused as children (Bird and Davis, 2004; Hawkins, 2005; Hill, 2004). Most see it as a traumatic experience, and a source of dissociation and part-selves, about which theory is evolving rapidly (Coffeng, 2002; Mearns, 1999; Prouty, 2002; Rutherford,

2007; Warner, 2001, 2005), although research remains sparse (Gavin Wolters, 2008; Morris et al., 2007).

The Child's Experience

Children begin life as integrated, unified beings, with a tendency, universal to all people, to 'maintain and enhance' their organism, to move towards being 'fully functioning' (Rogers, 1959). However, this requires unconditional positive regard and empathy from those around the child (particularly parents and carers), otherwise conditions of worth are likely to result in experience being distorted or denied (see Introduction). Sexual abuse can make this distortion and denial extreme.

Pauline

Pauline's addicted parents were unable to care for or protect her properly. She tried to do her own washing, but her clothes were often dirty, and she was taunted and isolated at school for being 'smelly'. Her self-structure developed to include the notion of '*Nobody wants me – I'm smelly,*' alongside her organismic yearning for contact. This increased Pauline's vulnerability to anyone who offered her time and attention, even if it was conditional. After she was sexually abused by a visitor to the house who told her that she was a 'little whore', she began to believe '*Nobody wants me – I'm a smelly little whore.*'

'Cultural' conditions of worth run through all areas of life, with groups valuing other groups according to differences like gender, class, age or religion. Unfortunately many adults value children negatively: they are extremely dependent for many years, are organismically energetic and expressive, and the task of bringing them up is a long and demanding one. Controlling and dismissive attitudes about children still persist in many cultures and can perpetuate an abusive climate. Although many conditions of worth are unique to a child's circumstances, an underlying societal 'given' is that due to their immaturity, their organismic experiences and frame of reference matter less than those of someone who is older. The feeling of 'not mattering' can be relative: *'I don't matter as much as the new baby'*; or, for children of abusive or neglectful parents, it might be absolute: *'I don't matter at all: Mum said she wished she'd never had me, now she's crying, and there's nothing to eat,'* leading them to feel that they don't matter to themselves either. When children experience sexual abuse they can develop extremely negative, even abusive self-regard, which can become so central to their self-concept that it influences many of their decisions and attitudes towards themselves.

Lesley

After a vicious street attack Lesley's anxiety and insomnia forced her to take time off from her demanding job. She couldn't understand why she couldn't hit the ground running and care for everybody as usual. When she was four, soon after her mother died, her aunt told her not to upset her Dad by crying. Her organismic needs as a grieving daughter were not acknowledged or valued, and her aunt scared her, so she stopped crying. Valuing her Dad's needs above her own became a condition of worth. Her aunt and uncle helped out by having Lesley to stay, which was valued by Dad, but not by Lesley, because her uncle abused her sexually. She hated this and felt ashamed about it, but never told her father, because she 'knew' that her feelings didn't matter as much as his.

With her therapist, Lesley experienced unconditional positive regard for all her feelings, and empathy for her four-year-old child's grief, confusion and horror at being sexually abused. Realising that her feelings meant a lot to her therapist challenged her 'not mattering', and gradually she began to matter to herself. She symbolised consciously the internalised message that she had lived by for years: '*I can't feel bad about anything difficult I experience in life, because it never matters as much as the grief that Dad experienced – so I can push myself and survive any pressure.*' As she valued herself more, she began to recognise when she needed to slow down.

Lesley's self-concept, embedded at age four, reinforced by emotional neglect and sexual abuse, was applied relentlessly in her life, even to her long working-hours. The trauma of the attack challenged her self-concept that she could survive anything, and stopped her functioning. (This harkening back to past, sometimes forgotten events can be a frequent response to trauma in the present – see Chapter 3.)

Aspects of the Abuser

Most abusers are known to a child (94 per cent according to recent research), and most sexual abuse happens in the home (NSPCC, 2007). Although many abusers like Lesley's uncle are married, and outwardly 'normal', they are not fully functioning and live 'double lives'. Their personality includes maladjusted needs, including sexual attraction to children, which often originates in their own childhood sexual abuse. Although figures are not definitive, the majority of those who suffer sexual abuse in childhood do not continue the cycle.

Active sexual abusers look for or take advantage of a gap in a child's care, which may be due to naivety on the part of the child's carers, or neglectful and abusive conditions already in place in a child's environment. They gain unsupervised access to children, in the majority of cases through ordinary family life; or otherwise through careful planning and grooming via, for example, voluntary or paid work, or social networking sites; and less frequently by accessing children in public places, or via organised 'rings'. They then use the children in various ways to gain sexual stimulation, and their attitudes can change, scarily and confusedly, from being affectionate and attentive to being threatening and terrorising. They exploit cultural or individual conditions of worth, which prevent children from retaliating, and to ensure silence and submission they may psychologically abuse using blame and humiliation, or instilling fear. In this sense they are like any other bully, but their needs are for sexual pleasure as well as domination.

Sheila I

In 1980, when public awareness about child sexual abuse was low, a middle-aged man used to walk in the park in the early evening, looking for young children playing on their own or in small groups, with no adults around. He chatted to them and gave them sweets and money, and the children got used to him, thinking that he was harmless but weird, they were safe in numbers, and made a game out of getting stuff off him. One evening he gave Sheila and her friend extra money and persuaded them to go into the toilets with him, for a game. Once inside, he forced Sheila's hand under his while he masturbated. When he finished, the girls ran away in shame and fear and never spoke to each other about it again. He didn't go back to the same park again for some time, and Sheila never dared play with her friends there again.

Abuser's Effect on a Child

Sexual abuse is a shocking and traumatic event: sexually abused children have physical and psychological contact with, and are used as an object by, someone with a major sexual and psychological maladjustment. They experience a flood of feelings and sensations, which often feel too strong and too numerous to manage. They are overpowered physically; they may sense that this person is dangerous, and their organismic desire to survive means that they comply. They probably have little knowledge about sex, so feel confused at what is happening. They may have inhibitions about genitals, so they feel shame and disgust; feel pain and repulsion at being touched; terrified that they might be killed; or have a desperate longing to flee. These feelings shock them into incongruence through denial and distortion. Some children begin to dissociate completely; they are jolted from experiencing life from their own frame of reference, into a traumatic awareness of having to focus on another's actions and feelings, and accommodate their perverted needs. Children can develop many conditions of worth as a result of trying to assimilate all these feelings at once, and untangling these in therapy can be a complicated process. They can respond organismically to the trauma with extreme fear and vigilance about the people around them, and isolate themselves to keep safe – responses that can become habitual.

At the time of the abuse, the abuser generally ignores a child's organismic experiences or forcibly stops them from expressing feelings. Equally, they may seem to enjoy the child expressing certain emotions and sensations, such as physical pleasure, but not others, which sets up yet other conditions. After they have finished, the abuser may completely switch their attitudes and suddenly deny anything happened at all; or they may distort what happened by describing it to the child as their fault, not a big deal, or something that they enjoyed and asked for; or they may act lovingly and call what happened a love affair. This makes an already terrible experience even more difficult for the child to make sense of, and the moral and social stigma means that they are not able to symbolise it accurately or to convey it to anyone. This benefits the abuser in maintaining secrecy, but it leaves the child negotiating a similar 'double reality' that can shift, from private abuse to a pretence of public normality, in a moment. Children themselves learn to switch too, and be deceitful about abuse, which can set up further negative self-regard, expressed internally as *'I'm a liar'*.

Abuser's Absence of Congruence, Empathy or Positive Regard

Abused children usually develop conditions of worth directly associated with the abuse, and sometimes these echo, underline or intertwine with already existing conditions from family or community. There are many powerful external influences working against their being able to tell their story at the time. Abusers usually coerce or threaten a child into silence, needing to maintain secrecy in order to protect themselves, and to allow continued access to the child or other children. If the child does tell, abusers almost always deny their abusing behaviour and, with only a child witness, abuse is impossible to prove without forensic evidence. General societal inhibitions about sex, which in turn contribute to 'cultural incongruence' (Hill, 2004) about sexual abuse, also help the abuser avoid detection. Added to this, an abused child's family background may be lacking in empathy and positive regard (sometimes only temporarily due to a family trauma of some kind) so children may feel that they have nobody to turn to, even if they could overcome other obstacles.

Terry I

Terry was physically and emotionally neglected by his alcoholic mother and stepfather. He was bullied in his street and viewed from the neighbourhood's frame of reference as an unwanted, strange child who should be grateful for any attention at all. He used to visit a neighbouring couple regularly who saw how desperate and isolated he was, and who fed him hot meals and offered him shelter. Unfortunately they also both sexually abused him: Terry often had to decide between going hungry and being abused.

Sheila II

Sheila was only in the park so often because she hated being at home. Her mother said that she was a 'mistake'; her brothers got away with bullying her. Feeling 'a nuisance', she played out on her bike in the park for hours in order to avoid the physical and emotional abuse at home. She knew that it was risky to go into the toilets with the weird man but, it had felt like an exciting game. Afterwards Sheila felt compelled to keep out of the house and keep moving, riding her bike round and round the streets on her own, in a dissociative 'trance'.

The Adult's Experience

All adult clients abused as children will experience varying levels of incongruence, examples of which are described below. They need what all clients need: a therapeutic relationship with a person who is congruent, empathic and accepting of their totality, including their abuse experience and its effects (for example problematic behaviour such as promiscuity, drug addiction or neglect of their own children), should they want to talk about them. They may:

- Isolate themselves and feel lonely and hopeless.
- Value themselves from others' frames of reference.
- Be involved in relationships that mirror this distorted focus on another's needs, rather than their own.

Therapy may be the first place where their frame of reference is acknowledged as important and their feelings valued. The therapist's job is not to go after memories of abuse, or change the client's thinking, but to create the conditions in a relationship where a person can experience changes in their self, which then allows denied material to enter awareness and be symbolised.

Remembering and Coping OK

Therapists must acknowledge that some adults sexually abused as children might have clear memories of sexual abuse, but have put them to the back of their mind as something they have got over, that did not affect them much, and they may not wish to seek therapy for the abuse.

Remembering and Distorting

Some people do remember being abused, but do not feel safe enough to explore it at first, for various reasons: perhaps, as with Shelia, they are ashamed that they *'made it happen'*, it only happened once, and they don't want to be a nuisance to the therapist. They may also have other, more pressing present-day issues to address, and in the process of doing so, can check out whether they feel safe enough to risk talking about the sexual abuse as well. They have consciously admitted the sexual abuse experiences into awareness, but have done so inaccurately, and thus given them a distorted symbolisation; through re-symbolising the abuse in a therapeutic relationship, they are able to assimilate their experiences into a changed, more congruent self-structure. Talking need not be the only kind of symbolisation.

Sheila III

Sheila initially came to therapy after a relationship breakup, feeling rejected, iso-lated and sometimes suicidal. As she gradually felt accepted by me, she came to accept herself more, for feeling claustrophobic indoors, for over-exercising, for being tongue-tied in sessions, for getting angry. She explored the sexual abuse last, and because she struggled with words, she symbolised the experience through drawing what had happened. She said, '*Because I took money, the abuse was my fault, so I've no right to feel bad about it*,' and '*It only happened once, so I shouldn't obsess about it*.' Doing the drawing helped her remember her organismic experi-encing during the abuse, and the image showed really clearly how small and pas-sive she was, compared with the man, who was relatively large and strong. With the support of my congruence, empathy and unconditional positive regard (UPR), her feelings of hate and disgust towards the abuser, previously not allowed into aware-ness, began to flow more freely, replacing her distorted feelings of self-hatred and self-disgust, and she realised that an innocent child could never have consented to the sexual act that she had drawn. By accepting her organismic experiences, she increased her congruence and a new self-concept formed: '*Although I was excited beforehand, when I thought it really was a game, I hated every minute of the sexual abuse bit, and it wasn't my fault; it was the man who forced me to touch him.*'

Vaguely Remembering and Distorting/Denying

Some clients may vaguely remember something nasty happening in their childhood, but have such a dim memory of it that it does not mean much, in which case they have almost completely denied the abuse, but it is on the very edge of their awareness. This may mean living with troubling feelings, but not knowing their cause.

Freda

Freda was sexually abused from a very young age by a family acquaintance and she had completely dissociated memories of it. She did remember a time when adults were furious and disgusted with her, and she had felt ashamed and guilty ever

(Continued)

(Continued)

since, but could not remember what she had done wrong. After a while in therapy she began to remember that she had been abused, and she realised that as a young child, without the language or concepts to describe the abuse, she had tried through body language and play to tell someone about it. Her innocent attempt was received with such violent judgement that she never tried to tell anyone again, and she internalised the adults' view of her as morally corrupt.

If the judging adults had had more awareness about child sexual abuse, they might have seen Freda's 'acting out' for what it was, and intervened early on, perhaps preventing further abuse. However, their attitudes helped deepen her negative self-regard, and like many sexually abused children, she introjected the guilt, shame and responsibility that should have rested with the abuser.

Denying Memory, Distorting through (psychiatric?) 'Symptoms'

Sometimes clients distort their abuse experiences to the point that only certain sensations or emotions experienced during sexual abuse remain available to awareness, but they are attributed to something else. Many clients terrified during childhood sexual abuse experience insomnia, digestive problems and panic attacks in adult life, but these are medicalised as 'anxiety'; others who feel sad, hopeless and isolated may be described as 'depressed'. While there is truth of a kind in these diagnoses, 'treating' such clients for 'anxiety' or 'depression' will not be as helpful as letting them explore their feelings and in so doing discover what gave rise to them.

Nora

Nora's 'panic attacks' sometimes stopped her from leaving the house. Her father *'had a temper'* and she had *'always been a worrier'*. While trying to understand when she first started worrying, Nora remembered catching her father sexually abusing her brother when she woke up after a nightmare. He threw her back into bed, shouting at her to keep her mouth shut, or he'd give her something to scream about. She lay in bed terrified, till he went to sleep, with her heart racing and feeling that she couldn't breathe. *'The same as with the panic attacks.'* Nora had distorted her traumatic organismic experience of witnessing sexual abuse and her father's violent reaction, into a more acceptable self-concept of *'I'm a worrier'* and a memory that *'Dad had a temper'*, but the sensations of terror had resurfaced as unexplained bursts of panic and breathlessness, all her life. Her GP had reinforced this distortion by giving her a medical diagnosis. Once Nora had symbolised accurately in awareness what really had 'worried' her, she became more congruent, and her unexplained 'attacks' stopped.

Symbolising Abuse Experiences via the Body

The process of accurately symbolising the organismic experiences of abuse in therapy can mean clients re-experience physical as well as emotional pain; this may also depend on how a place reminds them of where the abuse occurred.

Maria I

Maria, who had been orally abused in a small attic, often experienced sensations of being suffocated and strangled whilst in confined spaces; and she could only experience the rage that she had felt, but hadn't dared express, when out walking in wild places.

Rogers described how, in 'unusual or perverse circumstances', an organism might 'actualise its potentiality for self-destruction (and) its ability to bear pain' (1963: 4). Sexually abused children experience events that often involve great pain, which they learn to tolerate in order to survive; and they can often experience self-destructive urges throughout their lives. Neuroscience finds that people try to soothe themselves physically during pain or trauma by releasing naturally occurring 'opioids', and sometimes people use external activities or substances to 'soothe' themselves.

Billy

When Billy remembered being abused he wanted both to damage his body and to feel release from cutting himself, and he used alcohol and illegal opiates to blot out his pain, as well as to express destructive self-regard via his body.

Denied Memory, Forgotten Abuse

Other clients have no inkling at all that they have ever experienced anything sexually untoward in their childhood, in which case they have managed to successfully deny awareness of their organismic experiences, and to develop a self-concept that includes nothing involving sexual abuse.

However, the behaviours they develop that help maintain their dissociated self-concept will probably have damaging effects in their lives.

> ### Stephen
>
> Stephen, a highly qualified professional from a wealthy background, found it very hard to express his emotions or form relationships. He had dissociated the abuse that he had suffered at boarding school so thoroughly that it only emerged after a year in therapy. At first, Stephen discussed himself as if from a distance and had little language for feelings, other than anxiety or numbness. Once he began to remember the abuse he very slowly accepted, understood and expressed more of his organismic experiencing.

Dissociating and Configurations of Self

Clients dissociate in different ways. Changes in a client's body language can be a sign that they are entering a 'trance-like state', or that a hidden self is present in the room. Warner (2005) describes a 'dissociated process' where abused children can move into states that 'diminish immediate experiences' as a response to trauma. She finds that alternate or multiple personalities in adulthood usually have their origin in early childhood abuse, and sometimes they emerge in a session.

> ### Sheila IV
>
> Sheila was silent, staring into space, as frequently happened. Sensing that she was anxious and uncomfortable, I gently asked if something was bothering her and if I could help in any way. She replied that I'd think she was mad if she told me. Sheila had asked for reassurance before about whether she was mad, and I responded again that she wasn't and that it was safe to tell me anything if she chose to. She told me that an angry young girl was in the room, shouting at her: '*Shut up! Get out of here! Get on the bike and ride really fast!*'
>
>   The girl often harassed Sheila in this way, only quietening down once they were moving. She didn't want to speak to me directly, so I asked Sheila to tell her that she was welcome in the room, and that I was grateful that she trusted me enough to let Sheila reveal her presence.

She seemed to be more a configuration of Sheila's self than an alternate personality, since she never addressed me directly. This configuration of self (Mearns, 1999) or part-self, had probably formed at the time of Sheila's sexual abuse, and had stayed at the same age, still flooded with many of the associated emotions, sensations and behaviours, as if she were experiencing them in present time.

Sheila V

Her terrified need to run from a predator and get outside, to use physical exercise at least to control something, were also feelings that adult Sheila experienced, but it was more acceptable to her self-concept that these feelings were symbolised in a younger self. The rigidity of her self-structure must have loosened up a little to enable her to symbolise this configuration of self to me, and once she did, both selves relaxed a little toward each other: the girl-self became less angry now that Sheila had accepted and acknowledged her in my presence, and Sheila felt less intimidated by her.

Anjali

Anjali was bullied and sexually abused by a female staff member when placed in a children's home after her parents died. Later in life, if she had not slept well, she heard a woman's voice telling her, '*You're rubbish,*' '*You ought to kill yourself,*' and '*You're bad for people.*' This was a vocal configuration of Anjali's self, imbued with the venom that others had directed towards her, and Anjali's own despair and self-hatred. As her self-regard became more positive, the voice became a whisper and eventually ceased.

The Therapist's Experience

A person-centred therapist aims to create an emotional climate wherein a client can experience lasting changes in their self. However, from a client's point of view, the therapeutic relationship could be fraught with danger, especially because some aspects of therapy, such as the superior power of the therapist and the secrecy of a one-to-one meeting, are similar to experiences of abuse. Considering the secrets, lies and pretence surrounding sexual abuse, an adult client might find it difficult to trust anybody, and might expect most relationships to be abusive. The therapist's seemingly caring attitudes could be a trick. Unfortunately some therapists can and do abuse clients, either unwittingly, through incompetence, or by knowingly exploiting their vulnerability, and so therapists must be careful not to re-abuse clients in any way. If therapists are consistent, open and congruent about who they are, how they work and what they offer, clients will be more likely to trust them.

To empathise with the pain that a sexually abused child has experienced, and understand the psychological damage that abuse may have caused, therapists need to develop their empathic awareness – 'as if one were the other person' (Rogers, 1959: 211) – about how life can be for a child, and how this can play out in adult life, especially as they may never hear the actual details of the abuse. If they can understand how the traumatic experience of sexual abuse can create a particular complexity to their client's incongruence (such as types of 'difficult process' (Warner, 2001)) they may become more sensitive to the nuances of their client's experiencing. Therapists need to value unconditionally all aspects of a person, including all the possible configurations of self that can emerge as a result of abuse, and empathise with all the feelings belonging to each, even if they are conflicting.

Such configurations are unique to each person and each experience, but they will hold many different feelings, and have different attitudes to other configurations. They might include:

- the part who trusts everybody;
- the part who is good at hiding the abuse;
- the part who went along with the abuse to protect others;
- the part who feels sorry for the abuser;
- the part who wanted the abuser's attention;
- the part who felt pleasurable sensations.

All are of equal importance, and the therapist's attitudes to each should be consistently empathic and accepting. Abusers may also have had part-selves that were less abusive, or kind and loving – indeed, the client may still love their abuser if they were a family member – and therapists need to accept unconditionally a client's positive feelings about some of them, especially as they may be very intertwined with a client's own part-selves.

Maria II

Although during childhood Maria was often terrified of her father's strength and his dissociative ability to numb his feelings whilst abusing her, a similar 'policeman-like' part of her emerged in therapy. This part, which was also strong and numb and felt positive towards her father, had successfully emulated him and had helped her survive the abuse. She continued to dissociate through 'numbness' in adult life, and although this limited her relationships, she felt very ambivalent about changing this configuration of self, as it counterbalanced her fearful self so well.

Developing Awareness

To work more effectively and ethically with any issue it is helpful if therapists develop greater awareness about it on a number of levels: contextual, psychological, theoretical, legal and ethical, as well as self and attitudinal. In the case of sexual abuse, first and foremost a therapist needs to be ready to value and empathise deeply with any feelings and material that the person who experienced it wishes to tell them about. To become more emotionally aware and be ready to empathise with and assist another in their journey, a therapist needs to sort out their *own* incongruence, conditions of worth, prejudices and values attached to abuse, and perhaps explore their own childhood abuse, if it occurred.

Many experiences denied to or distorted in awareness by therapists can create barriers and lead them to dismiss, avoid or not notice sexual abuse material tentatively raised by a client. They may believe that the person-centred approach will 'work' with any issue that a client brings so that there is no need to focus on their abuse. An underlying reluctance to talk about sex and children's sexuality; a general lack of understanding resulting from deficiencies in training; a limited knowledge of person-centred theory; an acceptance of cultural myths and misunderstandings relating to sex and sexual abuse; fear of being out of their depth or horrified by what they may hear; and/or cultural or religious inhibitions may either severally or together impede the ability of therapists to work effectively with clients who have been abused as children.

Student Counsellor

A student counsellor just beginning her placement brought to supervision a male client who, in their first session, disclosed an experience of sexual abuse by a male cleric. This shocked the counsellor, whose faith group disapproved of homosexuality and certain sex acts. She felt uncomfortable and guilty talking alone with a man about sexual matters and could barely believe that 'cleric abuse' occurred.

This may have led her to minimise the abuse, because she presented it as 'only a one-off, not horrendous or anything', and struggled to offer the core conditions, viewing the abuse conditionally and from her own frame of reference, and judging (incorrectly) the depth of her client's distress.

Explaining that a single abuse event can be extremely distressing and have long-term consequences (as in Sheila's experience), and that, regrettably, abuse can happen in any institution, including a religious one, the supervisor suggested reading material about the issue. She challenged the counsellor's 'cultural incongruence', questioning the ethics of discriminatory (conditional) regard.

She also supported the counsellor in seeking therapeutic support for herself, hoping that it might enhance her empathy and positive regard for a client's abused child part.

Mindful of the client's needs, the supervisor suggested that he was referred to a counsellor who felt competent and congruent around the issue of sexual abuse. Later, with her consultant supervisor, she explored how best to raise the relevant issues with the training organisation and/or the placement provider.

Legal and Ethical Issues

Given that one in six clients could potentially bring the issue of sexual abuse to therapy, it is essential that therapists understand their legal and ethical responsibilities, particularly as regards child protection. The limits of confidentiality depend on a number of factors such as the therapist's ethical framework, their work setting and its organisational protocols and the age of the client. Clients can only make an informed choice about whether to disclose information about sexual abuse if they know exactly how confidential the therapy is, who the therapist might (or must) inform, and under what circumstances, and who else might see their records.

Needing Supervision for Self and Others

It is also important for therapists to explain their need for supervision and the protection that it can afford their client. Many abused children learn to take emotional or physical care of the abuser or their family, and often grow into adults who care for others, but not themselves. It can be a huge relief when the therapist explains how they (and the client) are looked after and monitored by supervision, thus explicitly refusing to add themselves to the client's (probably long) list of people that they already support. By showing that they too can acknowledge their own needs, and organise how to get some of them met, the therapist may encourage a client to feel that it is possible and permissible for them to do the same. Also, the therapist is clearly identifying a third person who could protect the client if they felt abused again in therapy.

For therapists working with adults who have been abused as children, supervision with someone who understands about sexual abuse is essential. The process of working with someone who brings to awareness denied-abuse experiences can be demanding as well as rewarding. Hearing how sexual predators seem to enjoy causing trauma and pain to vulnerable young people can challenge a therapist's understanding of the actualising tendency. Empathising with a client describing abuse – entering the client's world 'as if' they were the client themselves – can be to enter into some distressing scenarios.

> ### Katya
>
> As a child, Katya was sexually abused at night by her father and desperately tried to stop him in her childish way by putting on extra clothes in bed. Her strategy did not work, nor did her mother pick up on these signals. During the day she felt constant fear of the nights and extreme isolation, and at night she felt 'annihilated' every time the abuse happened. As an adult she relived these feelings in sessions: although her therapist showed a little of her own distress and anger on behalf of Katya's child-self, she did not want to overload adult Katya with her feelings, so she explored and offloaded them with her supervisior.

Sometimes people's experiences of abuse and the consequent negative self-regard that develops can lead them to become involved with abusive partners, who could themselves be a danger to children. The painful awareness of this risk may first become symbolised through therapy, and sometimes the supervisor can see it most clearly.

Tanesha

Tanesha suspected that her estranged husband was accessing internet child pornography, yet she allowed her young daughter to see him regularly, reassuring her therapist that he would never harm her. Her therapist accepted her judgement, but felt uncomfortable somehow, and voiced his unease to his supervisor.

The supervisor agreed with and reinforced the therapist's concerns, suggesting that because of Tanesha's own sexual abuse as a child, her awareness of risk about her daughter might still be distorted to some extent. The therapist woke up to the need to ask Tanesha more searching questions about her daughter's safety.

This can be difficult because it entails stepping outside the role of therapist and making a third person the focus of concern. It is important to explain this to the client so that the therapeutic work is not compromised, for example: 'I'm a bit worried about your daughter and I'm finding that I can't just carry on with the counselling without checking something out with you.'

Awareness of Power and Autonomy in Contracting and Ending

For Rogers, the actualising tendency moves a person 'toward autonomy and away from ... control by external forces' (1959: 196). Sadly, sexual abuse robs a child of autonomy, and therapists, who carry a great deal of emotional power and associated conditions of worth invested in their role, need to tread very carefully. Developing a collaborative process throughout the relationship, and particularly during contracting and ending, may counteract a client's powerlessness, sometimes offering the first opportunities to exercise personal power.

Terry II

At the end of a first session with Terry I said that I would like to work with him, and asked: 'Would you like to come back? You don't have to decide now; you can go away and think about it.' At first, Terry, a compliant patient with his GP, was unsettled and replied, 'I don't know. What do you think?' When I repeated that it was up to him to decide, that he knew better than me what he could cope with, he made his decision, and said later that it had helped him feel more confident.

The client will know from their organismic experience – of increasingly congruent self-concept and positive self-regard – when they are ready to end the relationship. However, endings often occur due to organisational constraints rather than client choice or therapeutic readiness, possibly leaving the client feeling helpless and abandoned. The therapist's power to 'send them away' can be experienced as mirroring the abuser or the family 'closing down' to the child, and negative self-regard can resurface. Therapists need to be congruent throughout about the implications of very short-term contracts with sexually abused clients, who may feel safer in a longer-term relationship.

Conclusion

Living through childhood sexual abuse can be a very difficult and frightening experience, and keeping memories at bay throughout childhood and adulthood is hard work. It diverts a person's energy, which could be better employed in life-enhancing activity. Sexual abuse can deeply damage a person's self-concept, causing repercussions in many relationships. So, if someone is lucky enough to meet a person-centred therapist who acknowledges the existence of sexual abuse, is well-informed about the issue and emotionally able and willing to work with it – and who works ethically and congruently with appropriate support for themselves – they will usually take the risk and get some help. If the client experiences an accepting and empathic therapeutic relationship with such a person, and begins the healing and empowering process of psychological change, they may then begin the risky process of bringing experiences of sexual abuse into awareness and of dealing with all the hidden feelings associated with them.

Further Reading

Detailed reading of any of the chapters and papers listed in the reference section will be helpful. In his 1959 paper, Rogers applies his theory of personality change to the relationships of parents with their children (p. 242). Some of his theories explain the actions of abusers and victims. His definition of dissociation within a deteriorating relationship, of 'almost complete incongruence ... between a person's experience, its cognitive meaning (symbolization), and its expression', can be applied to both in child sexual abuse (p. 237). When Rogers explained defensive behaviours with an example of someone saying 'I am pure, but you are trying to make me think filthy thoughts,' he referred to a typical distortion employed by sexual abusers when they project the responsibility for their actions onto their victims (p. 229).

Warner cites three types of difficult process, 'fragile', 'dissociated' and 'psychotic', which can be caused by sexual abuse trauma. She suggests that there are many types of difficult process, and advises that therapists offer simple rather than complex empathic responses to clients in these mind states. Prouty's and Coffeng's ideas about contact are helpful if working with a dissociating client. Mearns' ideas about configurations of self are relevant to abuse trauma: the resulting enforced incongruence can sometimes force part-selves underground, which then emerge in therapy. The National Society for the Prevention of Cruelty to Children (NSPCC) has produced a great deal of useful contemporary British research. Figures from ChildLine gathered since 1986 show the changing trends in incidence, prevalence and reporting of child sexual abuse.

References

Bird, M. and Davis, E. (2004) 'Making sense of monsters: Working therapeutically with women and children who have experienced sexual violence', in G. Proctor and M.B. Napier (eds), *Encountering Feminism: Intersections between Feminism and the Person-Centred Approach*. Ross-on-Wye: PCCS Books, pp. 191–206.

Cawson, P., Wattam, C., Brooker, S. and Kelly, G. (2000) *Child Maltreatment in the United Kingdom: A Study of the Prevalence of Child Abuse and Neglect*. London: National Society for the Prevention of Cruelty to Children (NSPCC).

Coffeng, T. (2002) 'Contact in the therapy of trauma and dissociation', in G. Wyatt and P. Sanders (eds), *Roger's Therapeutic Conditions: Evolution, Theory and Practice*, Vol. 4. *Contact and Perception*. Ross-on-Wye: PCCS Books, pp. 153–67.

Freud, S. (1896) *The Aetiology of Hysteria*. The Standard Edition of the Complete Psychological Works of Sigmund Freud, Vol. 3 (1893–9) Early Psycho-Analytic Publications. London: Vintage, pp. 187–221.

Gavin Wolters, M. (2008) 'Counseling adult survivors of childhood institutional abuse: A phenomenological exploration of therapists' perceptions and experiences in Ireland', *Person-Centered & Experiential Psychotherapies*, 7 (3): 185–99.

Hawkins, J. (2005) 'Living with pain: Mental health and the legacy of childhood abuse', in S. Joseph and R. Worsley (eds), *Person-Centred Psychopathology: A Positive Psychology of Mental Health*. Ross-on-Wye: PCCS Books, pp. 226–41.

Hill, M. (2004) 'Woman-centred practice', in G. Proctor and M.B. Napier (eds), *Encountering Feminism: Intersections between Feminism and the Person-Centred Approach*. Ross-on-Wye: PCCS Books, pp. 221–32.

Kinsey, A., Pomeroy, W., Martin, C. and Gebhard, P. (1953) *Sexual Behavior in the Human Female*. Philadelphia, PA: Saunders.

Mearns, D. (1999) 'Person-centred therapy with configurations of self', *Counselling*, 10 (2): 125–30.

Morris, M., Turner, R. and Rolfe, G. (2007) 'A collaborative inquiry between a person-centered therapist and a client: Working with an emerging dissociated "self"', *Person-Centered & Experiential Psychotherapies*, 6 (3): 78–111.

National Society for the Prevention of Cruelty to Children (NSPCC) (2007) *Calls to ChildLine about Sexual Abuse (ChildLine Casenotes)*. London: NSPCC.

Prouty, G. (2002) 'Pre-therapy: An essay in philosophical psychology; Pre-therapy as a theoretical system; The practice of pre-therapy', in G. Wyatt and P. Sanders (eds), *Roger's Therapeutic Conditions: Evolution, Theory and Practice*, Vol. 4. *Contact and Perception*. Ross-on-Wye: PCCS Books, pp. 51–3.

Rogers, C.R. (1959) 'A theory of therapy, personality, and interpersonal relationships, as developed in the client-centered framework', in S. Koch (ed.), *Psychology: A Study of a Science*, Vol. 3. *Formulations of the Person and the Social Context*. New York: McGraw-Hill, pp. 184–256.

Rogers, C.R. (1963) 'The actualizing tendency in relation to "motives" and to consciousness', in R. Jones (ed.), *Nebraska Symposium on Motivation*. Lincoln, NB: University of Nebraska Press, pp. 1–24.

Rutherford, M.C. (2007) 'Bearing witness: Working with clients who have experienced trauma – Considerations for a person-centered approach to counselling', *Person-Centered & Experiential Psychotherapies*, 6 (3): 153–68.

Warner, M. (2001) 'Empathy, relational depth and difficult client process', in S. Haugh and T. Merry (eds), *Rogers' Therapeutic Conditions: Evolution, Theory and Practice*, Vol. 2. *Empathy*. Ross-on-Wye: PCCS Books, pp. 181–91.

Warner, M. (2005) 'A person-centered view of human nature, wellness and psychopathology', in S. Joseph and R. Worsley (eds), *Person-Centred Psychopathology: A Positive Psychology of Mental Health*. Ross-on-Wye: PCCS Books, pp. 91–109.

PART TWO

Emotional Reactions to Life Events

5

PERSON-CENTRED THERAPY WITH PEOPLE EXPERIENCING DEPRESSION

WHEN YOU CAN'T JUST SNAP OUT OF IT

KIRSHEN RUNDLE

What is Depression?

I could find little in person-centred literature specifically on 'depression' and, in trying to define its particular characteristics, I was surprised at the range of emotions and feelings experienced by those of my clients who describe themselves, or have been described by others, as 'depressed'. These include:

> numbness, lethargy, stuckness, unhappiness, hopelessness, helplessness, despair, isolation, anger, guilt, shame, worthlessness, loneliness ...

What is common, however, is a sense of being unable to cope with ordinary life or to ask for help, and that no one will understand what is wrong or be able to help anyway. Often there are also feelings of shame at failing to meet their own or others' expectations of their various roles, achievements or obligations. Person-centred theory might describe this perception of failure as part of having an external locus of evaluation. But it is undoubtedly exacerbated by current public attitudes towards 'mental illness' and those who do not appear to be easily self-reliant. Despite this stigma, some people are tempted to seek help from experts who will cure their 'illness' (or chemical imbalance), but one of my worries about a diagnosis or label of 'depression' is that it pathologises the individual. An effect of this is that distressing events such as bereavement, divorce, job loss and work stress become classed as mental health problems requiring medical 'cures', when they are actually part of what it is to be human.

This 'medicalisation' of misery does nothing to change the actual situation that the person finds themselves in (drugs cannot bring back a loved one who has died, for example). It also diverts someone from exploring social factors or life events that may have led to the unhappiness in the first place and their satisfaction (or otherwise) with the way that they are living their lives. In person-centred terms they are denied the chance to experience events fully or to investigate the extent to which their self-concept matches the flow of their experiencing (Rogers, 1959). The person-centred belief in the uniqueness of the individual also precludes, for me, the idea of there being a condition, let alone a mental illness, called 'depression'. People react differently to similar events, so aggregation and categorisation of 'symptoms' into a fixed entity cannot possibly capture the nuances and idiosyncrasies of all stories and experiences. We must be guided by each client as the expert in what hurts and what heals (Rogers, 1961: 11–12) in order best to facilitate an easing of the pain.

How Can Person-Centred Therapy Help?

Person-centred therapy is well placed to help people experiencing 'depression'. It is not directive, will not force people to 'do' things or to 'get better' when they can barely get through the days, and the therapist will be brave enough to accompany clients into the darkest and bleakest of places. That willingness to join clients in their despair can mark an end to their sense of loneliness and isolation and can be the start of the journey back. It can also help them to see that they can be understood and that their pain can be seen by someone else. When people are in such a profound state of isolation or deep unhappiness, struggling with feeling stuck, shame, guilt and despair, empathic understanding is crucial. Unconditional positive regard can help those who are frightened to allow themselves to feel powerful emotion, whether that is connected to an event or to a challenge to a self-structure. Therapist congruence enables clients to explore their own bleak landscapes freely without needing to worry about damaging the therapist. Such transparency and genuine presence in the therapeutic relationship may also assist the emergence of the client's own courage as part of the encounter. If the therapist communicates all these qualities to the vulnerable client, then healing is facilitated.

In the person-centred approach, techniques are seen as irrelevant, or even a hindrance. The relationship *is* the therapy; it is a dialogue and is co-created (Schmid, 2006: 250–4) by therapist and client. Given that depression is often marked by a feeling of an inability to be in a relationship, the therapeutic encounter could be a significant chance to experience being connected with someone again. By creating a safe, accepting environment where a client feels heard and understood, a therapist can help a client to explore other possibilities and other explanations for things (Propositions XVII and XIX, Rogers, 1951: 438–522). That may then allow them to become more open to the flow of their experiencing and to explore the views they have of themselves (Rogers, 1959). Whilst, for a person-centred therapist, challenges will always be tentative and will come from the client's frame of reference, they are still part of the process. When trying to understand empathically what is going on for our client we may, at times, get a sense of something behind the words and so it makes sense to flag that up to them. If it means nothing to them, we let it go; if it resonates, they may explore it (Propositions XI and XVII). Any challenge is usually brushed away or not even heard until the client feels that it is relevant or that they can face allowing it to become symbolised (Proposition XI). At all times, however, the therapeutic process must operate from within the client's frame of reference. When this does not happen a client can be left feeling even more vulnerable and in pain, as in the following story of Notty, a young man who had been very depressed during his time in prison.

Notty

At his fifth session Notty was feeling happy and started to talk about plans for after his release. We stayed with that for a while but then he heard a fracas outside the room. He went to intervene but the officers told him to 'Fuck off!' and he felt bad that he was unable to protect his friend. Instead of staying with that or letting him direct us back to his 'happy mood', I referred to when he had previously felt bad about not being able to protect his brother. That took him straight back to something that he found incredibly painful and that he had struggled each week to deal with. He was plunged into misery again and, the next week, said how long it had taken him to come back from it.

Not for the first time, I should have kept my mouth shut! The only positive thing is that Notty felt able to tell me honestly how badly he had been affected by what had happened. This contrasts with a previous session where we had stayed with some happy feelings that he was experiencing. Then he had used the session well but had left feeling positive and that feeling had stayed with him too. It showed me how powerful the effect is of either staying with someone (in pain or joy) or pushing them somewhere else.

When there's a Reason

An accumulation of life events can result in a person feeling depressed even though they feel that they 'should' be able to cope with what has happened. Consider the people below in terms of the distress suffered and the road to some healing.

Robert

Robert had been to see his doctor because he was tired all the time, found it difficult to show any interest in his children or grandchildren and no longer even wanted to work in his garden. All these things had been such a source of joy, pride and relaxation to him in the past. The extent of his hopelessness worried him because he had a wife and family to care for. He was grateful when the doctor prescribed antidepressants and his wife told their daughter, Cassie, stressing that it was nothing to be ashamed of and that the tablets would soon correct the chemical imbalance that was causing her dad's 'illness'. Cassie knew what had been going on in her dad's life over the previous year or so. He was recovering from prostate cancer; two of his close friends and his brother-in-law had died; another friend had been diagnosed with lung cancer; he had money worries; and one of Cassie's sisters was relying heavily on her mum and dad for support following the breakup of her marriage. Added to this she knew that her dad was increasingly worried about how forgetful her mum was becoming and about who would care for her if he died. As far as Cassie could see, suffering the pain of loss and worry was not the same thing as 'illness' or chemical imbalance and she could not see that tablets would change things. So she hesitantly suggested that he seek some counselling help. A few weeks later he said that he had done just that and, to his surprise, it had helped enormously. Before, he had always held his worries to himself because he didn't want to upset Cassie's mum or any of his family. He was supposed to be the 'man of the house': the person others could rely on. The counsellor, he said, 'allowed' him to talk about what caused him such sadness and concern when he felt he could, instead of asking lots of questions or telling him what he should be doing to get better. He liked this as he had been worried about staying in control if he was going to be a 'mental patient'. He said that he was arriving at some acceptance and peace about things.

The facts of Robert's life had not changed; pain, sadness and loss remained, but bringing things into the open helped him realise that these things were reason enough for at least some of his distress and other 'symptoms'. Robert's paralysing fear of the pain shifted as well as his need to be strong for all those around him, both of which lifted a huge burden from him. He slowly started to take part in his life and to get out into his beloved garden again. He also felt able to discuss plans with Cassie and her sisters for the long-term care of their mother. In some ways Robert was fortunate. He was retired so he did not have the additional pressure of a job to worry about. He was able to take the time he needed to go at his own pace in the exploration of just what there was at the root of his feelings of lethargy, hopelessness and the wish to withdraw from taking part in life or being with people.

Robert was enabled to arive at some acceptance of the things that had happened, and were happening, sad as they were. He also came to accept that these things could account for his distress and debilitation, rather than there being things that he 'should have been able to deal with' as a strong man. He no longer felt that he needed to allocate the distress and other 'symptoms' to his own 'weakness' or to a 'chemical imbalance' or illness. For Robert, this was the extent of the work that he needed to 'do'. I see this as a positive aspect of person-centred therapy in that no attempt was made to direct him to explore aspects of his self-structure to do with why he felt the need always to act as strong, reliable; why he originally saw it as 'weak' to be so affected by sad events or stress; whether he could become more accepting of other aspects of himself and could challenge the expectations that he demanded of himself. Yes, maybe if his self-structure had been different he would not have become so debilitated by his distress because he could have allowed himself really to experience his sadness as it happened – he could have been open to the flow of his experiencing. But he was a product of his time – of the traditional British attitude of men needing to be strong, hold a stiff upper lip, be head of the house. That had served him and his family well and he saw no reason to consider changing it. At the age of seventy-five, however, in the face of such overwhelming struggles, he had finally allowed himself to be a bit kinder to himself and to relax the pressure, just a little.

Daverne I

Daverne had three children aged six, eleven and thirteen years and had found it increasingly difficult to cope since her husband had killed himself a year ago. She felt guilty about the frequent arguments that they had, stressing that he had been a good man and that she loved him. This added to the guilt that she felt for failing to protect her children sufficiently. She had divorced the father of her two oldest children after she discovered that he had been sexually abusing their two-year-old daughter. Being a 'good mother' had always been very important to her and was even more so now that she was the only one left to look after them. She believed that she had contracted this depression and that it was entirely external to her. She saw counselling as her 'opportunity to work hard', explore her sadness and 'get back to normal' for her children.

In our second session I tentatively asked if she thought that the events from the past might have had some bearing on how unhappy she was but she was completely nonplussed to think that it might be so. I let it go but realised that I had slipped into my own frame of reference and was in danger of pursuing my own agenda for her 'recovery'. So we spent most of the session on her distress and about how she had always felt responsible for making sure that everyone was happy and cared for. She said that she had loved having a 'normal' life with her second husband and wanted to talk of happy times.

She would often start our sessions in great distress but, working at her pace and focusing on the areas of her choosing, she invariably found her own way through the enveloping sadness and came to some different perspective. If I had tried to direct her or suggest ways of coping or tried to deny her reality I do not think that it would have worked, even though I often felt that she was asking me for answers. On more than one occasion I found myself feeling that she would be better suited to a more directive form of therapy! I also confess that I became bored by the repetitive nature of her process where we revisited the same things time after time.

As ever, my supervisor offered me vital help and insights. She suggested that my boredom might be a reflection of Daverne's and that helped me become more accepting of it in myself. This then seemed to free me up to become more present for her and to stay with the awfulness of her pain, frustration and stuckness. She also challenged whether I was really offering unconditional positive regard if I found it difficult to accept my client's understanding of her reality, which was that she had been 'invaded' by an illness and was failing as a mother because of it. My ability to be able to experience my client's world as if it were my own would be hindered if I moved out of her frame of reference. My supervisor reminded me of those instances where I had shown empathic responding – or not – which helped reinforce the value of congruent self-awareness by highlighting those times when I had felt tempted to 'rescue'. This helped me remember what they had felt like and watch out for them in subsequent sessions.

A way of being that has developed over many years can be deeply rooted in a person's sense of self and, when difficulties occur, tends to be clung onto ever more tightly (Proposition XVI). Confirming data is assimilated and conflicting data being ignored (Propositions X–XIV), possibly to deliver some sense of certainty in an unpredictable or unhappy world. This can only add to a sense of stuckness or paralysis. Therapy can then feel circular where clients visit the same story in the same way week after week, as if they are unable even to consider that there might be a way through the pain or a way of feeling differently. Being immobilised in misery, however, may serve as a protective or anaesthetising function against the pain it is assumed will come when reality is addressed – whether that be acceptance of a loss, or the fear, uncertainty and awareness of distress for self or others that may accompany change.

Daverne II

Daverne's sixth session marked a turning point. She was particularly distressed, full of hopelessness and fear. She was hearing the voice of 'a devil' that told her to have the Social Services take her children away because she had to commit suicide. She was confused too, saying that she would never give them up or kill herself. This was the first time that she had mentioned thoughts of suicide. Today, however, she did not know how to carry on and she missed her husband so much that she wanted to be with him again. At the same time though, she felt distraught and terrified at what her children would go through if she did kill herself, and spoke again of just wanting 'this illness' to go but that it was so powerful and 'went all the way through' her.

As had happened before I started to feel overwhelmed myself and to feel that I was out of my depth. This time, however, I recognised it as her distress which somehow kept me grounded and I trusted that she would bring herself to a resolution again. Then, for some reason, I followed up on a strong urge to ask her how much of her fear and distress about the children was related to the experience that she herself had had when she found her husband's body after his suicide. It had a dramatic effect. She looked at me for the first time that week and said that it was connected. I then found myself asking – very gently – whether she felt that it would help to talk about it and she said that it would, as she had never had the chance to do so before. The rest of the session was extremely traumatic for her as she went into graphic details of the lead-up to his suicide, what it was like to find his body, details of what it looked like then and later when she had formally to identify the body, and her mixed emotions since his death. Although difficult and painful for her it also acted as a catharsis and she finished the session saying that she felt calm and peaceful.

In the following session, she said that she no longer wanted to 'rake over all this stuff'; she wanted 'to move on and finish grieving'. Although positive, she was afraid of slipping back into the depression again. She said that she now felt that each 'chunk' of the depression could be explored to see how much of it was, in fact, to do with elements of herself or her life. The fact that one 'chunk' had already been worked through had created a space to assess other things differently – she was already starting to accept that her marriage had not been perfect, that her husband had tried to control her and had unpredictable rages. She said how much lighter her life was without him and was angry about what he had put her and the children through.

Her continuing recovery was evident in our final review session. She was feeling increasingly able to 'take up the reins' of her life but was also allowing herself to 'take it slowly'. She said that she had not heard the voice of her 'devil' since that session in which she had talked about her husband's suicide. She said that she knew that she would not give up her children but occasionally still worried whether she would always be a 'good enough' mother.

My work with Daverne was a key example for me of the strength of the person-centred approach; of how the client really can be trusted to have the resources within to find the solutions that work for her and how the therapist's only role is to facilitate each client's unique actualising process. It was humbling to see the power of 'being' rather than 'doing' the therapist conditions and to recognise when congruent awareness of something comes from an intuitive, empathic response to another's frame of reference. The importance of feeling valued and known in the relationship with one's supervisor is also essential in offering a safe place to explore issues that may be difficult.

For Robert and Daverne, the balance of their actualising processes was restored once their immediate distress had been explored. Their forces of social mediation were such that they could continue to actualise in the ways that worked for them; and those aspects of their self-concepts that had formed part of the stress in their distress were actually also sources of comfort, pleasure and self-esteem when their lives were manageable. Whether the experience of allowing themselves to be open to the flow of their experiencing and addressing things from a different perspective will lead to further work, I do not know. But that is part of what Rogers describes as the self being a process of becoming rather than a fixed entity. It is also related to Mearns and Thorne's concept of configurations of self – different aspects of self, any one of which can come to the fore at different times and in different circumstances (Mearns and Thorne, 2000: 101–119). Robert's view of himself as a 'good husband, father and provider' and Daverne's view of herself as a 'good mother and protector of her children' were key aspects of selves that, once re-established and functioning well, played a great role in their recoveries.

But What about When Nothing's Wrong?

There are those who cannot understand why they are feeling so dreadful, so lacking in energy, so miserable, so hopeless. Some may not even see a problem until they experience an actual 'breakdown'. In these cases, it may well be that, after struggling to hold onto a self-concept that becomes increasingly rigid as experience contradicts it (Proposition XVI), the discrepancies between the two become so great (Proposition XII, XIII, XV) that the person eventually has to give up the fight. In an odd sort of way, this can be the start of the healing process. In that giving up comes a freedom, a release, an openness to looking at things differently. The next two stories are examples of people who, with hindsight, saw that things had been wrong for a long time but who came into counselling rather by surprise.

Pradeep

Pradeep was a medical student from a high-achieving family and played squash at county level. He could not understand why he didn't want to be alive anymore but repeated suicide attempts meant that he was hospitalised and referred for counselling. This worried him because of the impact that it might have on his future career. He told me that he wanted 'to look at family issues' that were not connected to his 'mental illness'. It was as if his 'illness' was being handled by the medical team and the rest of his life was being explored in counselling. Pradeep had initially attended counselling without much hope that it would help, as he told me later. Perhaps he had started at an earlier stage of the process than I had thought (Rogers, 1961). At Stages 1 and 2 people are unwilling or unable to own or communicate self and initially feel threatened by close relationships. Most people come into therapy at about Stage 3 and are more open to exploring self, though as an object at first, still unable to recognise or own difficult feelings.

Pradeep slowly told me about his family and his father's death when he was twelve years old. His mother appeared to rely on him for emotional support as his elder siblings had already left home and there were often arguments between his mother and her in-laws. This was a struggle for him as he felt disloyal if he suspected that he had given me the impression that his family relationships were less than perfect or even difficult.

A few months before his first overdose two friends at university had been involved in a fight and one had been seriously injured. There was tension between the two with each blaming the other for the incident and Pradeep found himself trying to act as mediator. The fight also reminded him of something that had happened when he was sixteen years old, which made him feel, he said, that he had let himself and his family down. This brought back the feelings of worthlessness and unreliability that he had felt then, but he was adamant that he had coped with it and was doing well in his studies and socially.

I remarked that this was similar to the situation that he found himself in at home and he couldn't ever make it all okay there either. He said that it resonated with him and that he failed people, but that he resented feeling this pressure. He then criticised his family and friends for failing to give him support when he needed it. He also said that his illness meant that he could no longer rely on himself and that it was terrifying not to be able to guarantee his own safety. By this time he was about to be discharged from hospital and he decided, reluctantly, to return to his family home for a while before returning to university. After two weeks back home he said that he had developed a different feeling about his family; that this time they had been there for him; and that, for all that was difficult, theirs was a loving family. He said that he had come to love them *because* of the way that they were, rather than *in spite* of it. He said that counselling had given him the courage to look honestly at the way that his family lived and the effects that this had on him. Once he realised that the whole edifice did not come tumbling down he developed a more realistic view of them, and them in relation to him, which was nourishing and nurturing. He was surprised that this had happened and now wanted to explore feelings of worthlessness, looking first at what happened when he was sixteen. He describes himself as 'a work in progress!'

The next story illustrates the long and painful process of discovery that a person can go through on a journey through depression, and it is told jointly from the client's and the therapist's perspective. Person-centred theory argues that the self-structure is developed and then sustained or changed through being in relationship with others. People who feel depressed are often lacking in close or intimate relationships and can feel terribly alone. For someone to have the chance really to connect with a therapist can be the start of healing and the start of re-engaging with people again after a period of isolation or alienation. Leonie was a busy person, always surrounded by people. It was only when she came into counselling following a breakdown that she realised how lonely she was and how much she craved intimacy. Her story starts with her words about the night of her breakdown.

Leonie I

I hung up the phone, angry about this latest row with mum, and knew. In that moment I just knew I couldn't do it any longer. I felt emptiness and yet ... something else ... what was it? Yes ... how very odd ... I felt elated. Pain would come later I suspected but, for now, the knowledge that I was no longer going to struggle brought with it lightness and relief. I told my husband I could not pick up the children from their tennis lessons, was not going to my school governors' meeting and that, whether or not his business dinner was important, he would have to stay at home until the children were sorted out. I didn't even feel guilty! My husband had never seen me so calm and still. I asked him to take me to the doctor's because I knew I couldn't drive myself. The doctor was about to leave but invited us into the surgery. As soon as we sat down, the tears started. I was shocked; I couldn't remember the last time I had cried. The release of emotion was so comforting but also worrying. What right did I have to take up the doctor's time with this ridiculous sobbing? People were starving in Africa. I had a perfect life. Loving husband, wonderful children, comfortable lifestyle, active in the local community. The doctor asked about my life and I stressed how lucky I was, that I liked my busy life. I said I was pleased the children took part in so many different activities, and I enjoyed the freedom I had during the day which enabled me to be Chair of the school's governing body, to go to the gym, to play tennis and to meet my friends for lunch. I said I enjoyed giving dinner parties for my husband's business contacts and I was grateful that his high-powered job meant I was not forced to seek paid employment myself. I said I saw it as my role to be main carer for the children because my husband worked long hours and often went abroad on business trips. I said I was happy with the decision we had jointly made for me to give up my career as a lawyer when we had children. So why was I feeling like this? The doctor said I was depressed, prescribed antidepressants and referred me to a counsellor.

I was so ashamed, embarrassed at needing help. Exhausted too. But I never missed my counselling. Once I even arrived with wet hair. I'd washed it but knew I could either dry it OR go to counselling. I couldn't do both. All my previous 'busyness' meant I'd never had time to consider whether I was happy. When I stopped I realised, with a shock, how desperately lonely I had been for a long time; how much I longed for, and was lacking, close relationships. Gradually, we started to look at how I had always believed that being a wife and mother would bring me happiness and contentment so felt guilty and ashamed when it didn't. And how I believed I had never measured up to my own mum because of this. I felt guilty that I didn't always want to do the same things as my husband: sometimes I just wanted to read the Sunday papers instead of going out on the boat. I felt guilty for wishing he would spend time just being together. I took a big risk by telling my counsellor that I had sought intimacy through a number of extra-marital affairs and that I felt no guilt at all. I expected her to think really badly of me but all she did was to comment on what I did feel and the fact that I expected to be judged by her. Actually, I wanted her to reassure me that she didn't think badly of me but she didn't do that either.

This was indicative for Leonie of her life more generally. She constantly judged herself as failing and expected others to do the same. She spent a long time exploring her beliefs about how bad she was not to be grateful for her lifestyle and how bad she was to think negatively about her 'ideal' husband. My offering of acceptance and empathy, without trying to rescue her in any way, was a major challenge to her way of being. *'If I was okay even with that sin, then I might not be so bad in other ways and I might be able to make things better for myself.'* She has always shown courage in exploring whether there might be another way of thinking about things. So whilst it has been a slow process it has not felt to me like a stuck process. At certain times she appeared more vulnerable than at others. Then I have stayed absolutely with simply reflecting her words and feelings, which has enabled her to notice what does not feel right for her; at other times she has invited more challenge. She has made huge changes to her life over the last three years and has suffered greatly at times because of some of them. She has challenged the assumptions and conditions of worth that she had introjected from her parents about what makes a 'happy woman' and a 'good wife and mother' and has come to accept the value of the unique love and support that she gives to her family. This is evidence of her move towards developing an internal locus of evaluation.

Leonie had spent so long living a life that other people had told her was a fortunate one and one that would make her happy, that she had stopped hearing her own voice. She wondered if she even had her own voice anymore. But, in fact, it was her voice (the actualising tendency) that had cried out *'ENOUGH!'* and then created the time and space to look at what she was missing in her life: what was really important and had meaning for her. She realised with sadness and fear that her marriage was empty. Her seeking intimacy elsewhere was, she came to believe, her actualising tendency fighting against the trap that she felt herself to be in. Both she and her husband had had these huge expectations that marriage was the automatic route to happiness. But they had both kept themselves so busy that they never had to address whether they actually had a close connection. It took Leonie's breakdown for them both to decide that intimacy with each other was what they both wanted. Leonie's extra-marital affairs had offered her temporary sexual intimacy but never any real chance of more – again, she protected herself from becoming completely vulnerable as we must do when risking relating so closely.

Leonie II

I am still seeing my counsellor but came off the tablets after only a few months. They didn't seem to be doing anything and I was putting on weight. I decided I would rather be thin and miserable than fat and miserable! Over that time I have come to feel differently about many things, which has created surprise, pain and, overall, more happiness. I am more at ease with myself and with those close to me. My husband and I have fallen in love again and I am training to be an interior designer – something *I* have chosen that fits with *my* wishes.

Alongside the challenges to what she had always felt to be her truths, Leonie has had to discover what would fit into the place of her previous way of being. When nothing else presents itself as an option, it is understandable that original assumptions are grasped more tightly. Each new realisation became accepted then integrated for a while before she moved on to the next. Each time there was a plateau, we stayed with pure reflection in our sessions. Even paraphrasing was uncomfortable or glossed over until the time was right for the next move. Throughout our work together I have been able to see Leonie's view of herself changing and mirroring Rogers' seven stages of therapeutic process (Rogers, 1961). She has become more open to the flow of her experiencing and has come to own her feelings. Her courage has enabled her to take advantage of the therapeutic conditions, allowing her hold on her original self-concept to be loosened and for her to find a more growthful way of being.

When Suicide Seems the Only Answer

Sometimes people who are depressed feel so hopeless that the only solution that they see is to take their own lives. This can be a point of contention in the person-centred approach. If we genuinely believe that clients' actualising processes mean that they will always make the best choices for themselves, we must accept that this may include the choice to end their lives. Certainly, I have worked with people who present such a logical case for this choice that it does not seem wrong or even sad. It is true though that wanting to be dead seems different from wanting the pain to go away. In either case a person-centred therapist will stay with the client's reality in that moment. Just to have expressed this wish out loud and be heard in such a state of anguish may help a client to feel less alone and give a glimmer of hope. Or they may conclude that it is a fantastical idea and that they have no need to feel scared of the risk of killing themselves. I do not see it as my role to try and talk a client out of such a plan but I was also comfortable with the actions of a colleague who thought that her client was at risk and so spent the whole night just being with him, so he that knew that he was not alone. He was extremely grateful, saying that he was relieved and pleased to 'get another chance at life'. In contrast to some approaches that value professional detachment, the relationship between the therapist and the client is central to person-centred therapy.

There may be procedures at agencies that require counsellors to break confidentiality if they believe that a client is at risk of suicide. This is made clear to clients at the start of therapy and then again if the situation actually occurs. This takes some responsibility away from therapists but requires them to make an ethical choice before starting work there. Even if a therapist is not subject to such rules, I believe that, in the end, the decision to break confidentiality over this issue must remain a personal ethical choice for each therapist. In order to avoid confusion or further distress this position should be communicated to the client at the start of therapy and reiterated if need be. Furthermore, it should be presented to the client as an action that will be taken, not an issue for discussion.

As every situation is unique so it will generate a different feeling. Ultimately, then, I suggest that the appropriate response will always be the result of a unique judgement.

Conclusion

Some people have just one experience 'of depression'; others go through their lives suffering bouts of 'depression'. This is sad and, for some, might just be the way they are. Or, it might fit better with a person's worldview to consider their pain as an illness and that medication helps. Those truths cannot be disputed. It may be, though, that they have not had the opportunity to explore the development of an authentic self-structure balanced by the forces of social mediation in their lives.

Once clients allow themselves to consider an alternative worldview – even if they then reject it – their rigid hold onto their existing self-structure has loosened. This, together with feeling accepted, valued and heard, can help people experience a shift in their feelings of depression. I would not describe it as a 'cure' because: (a) it implies that it was a medical condition in the first place; and (b) it implies a movement from one fixed state to another that contradicts the person-centred position of the self as a process of becoming.

Person-centred therapeutic relationships do seem to help people free up their internal resources, so bringing about an easing of their pain and alienation that may also enable them to cope if they encounter future struggles. If therapy can help someone to explore which aspects of the self-structure are still helpful or have meaning for them, it must be useful and healing. It allows the client to remain as expert in their own process, to know what hurts and what helps and to direct the pace and focus of the therapeutic process. It enables them to find the 'coping strategies' that work for them at the same time as coming to an awareness of what particular events or aspects of self really mean for them.

Note

Client stories are based on work with actual clients but are fictional composites of two or more people.

Guide to Further Reading

Mearns, D. and Cooper, M. (2005) *Working at Relational Depth in Counselling and Psychotherapy*. London: Sage.

Isolation and a lack of relationship are often associated with feelings of depression. Focusing on a relational approach, this book explores how a therapist can enhance their practice.

Reeves, A. and Seber, P. (2007) *Working with the Suicidal Client*. British Association for Counselling and Psychotherapy (BACP) Information Sheet P7. Lutterworth: BACP.

Not person-centred specifically but useful to help in coming to a provisional, personal ethical position on suicide.

Sanders, P. and Tudor, K. (2001) 'This is therapy: A person-centred critique of the contemporary psychiatric system', in C. Newnes, G. Holmes and C. Dunn (eds), *This is Madness too: Critical Perspectives on Mental Health Services*. Ross-on-Wye: PCCS Books, pp. 147–60.

Sommerbeck, L. (2003) *The Client-Centred Therapist in Psychiatric Contexts: A Therapists' Guide to the Psychiatric Landscape and its Inhabitants*. Ross-on-Wye: PCCS Books.

These two works are about person-centred approaches to different forms of so-called psychopathology, including reference to understandings of 'depression'. They highlight ethical and philosophical tensions and possibilities for person-centred practitioners working in psychiatric and other contexts.

Worsley, R. (2007) 'Diagnosis, stuckness and encounter: Existential meaning in long-term depression', in R. Worsley and S. Joseph (eds), *Person-Centred Practice: Case Studies in Positive Psychology*. Ross-on-Wye: PCCS Books, pp. 98–114.

Beautifully evokes the circularity and stuckness of working with someone in a depression.

References

Mearns, D. and Cooper, M. (2005) *Working at Relational Depth in Counselling and Psychotherapy*. London: Sage.

Mearns, D. and Thorne, B. (eds) (2000) *Person-Centred Therapy Today: New Frontiers in Theory and Practice*. London: Sage.

Rogers, C.R. (1951) 'A theory of personality and behaviour', in C.R. Rogers, *Client-Centered Therapy*. London: Constable, pp. 481–533.

Rogers, C.R. (1959) 'A theory of therapy, personality and interpersonal relationships as developed in the client-centered framework', in S. Koch (ed.), *Psychology: A Study of Science*, Vol. 3. *Formulations of the Person and the Social Context*. New York: McGraw-Hill, pp. 184–256.

Rogers, C.R. (1961) 'A process conception of psychotherapy', in C.R. Rogers, *On Becoming a Person: A Therapist's View of Psychotherapy*. London: Constable, pp. 125–59.

Schmid, P. (2006) 'The challenge of the other: Towards dialogical person-centered psychotherapy and counselling', *Person-Centered & Experiential Psychotherapies*, 5 (4): 250–4.

6

ANXIETY AND PANIC

PERSON-CENTRED INTERPRETATIONS AND RESPONSES

RICHARD BRYANT-JEFFERIES

Anxiety and panic can be explained in terms of physiological processes and, from a behavioural perspective, the ways of managing these include teaching relaxation techniques and containing the symptoms that arise. We also know that certain prescription drugs can help to ease the symptoms, often as a short-term measure to help a person stabilise their anxiety. However, there are those for whom the outcome of a medical intervention is long-term prescribing. The difficulty with this is that if the cause is psychological rather than physiological/chemical, the initial problem may not be resolved and the removal of the medication could lead to symptoms returning. In addition, long-term prescribing can itself lead to dependence (chemical or psychological), which can in turn lead to the emergence of anxiety symptoms when medication is stopped or reduced.

Introducing a Person-Centred Perspective

Person-centred practitioners have a different approach. For us, dealing with anxiety and panic is not about managing a set of experiences but rather of genuinely and unconditionally accepting the person and responding to them empathically. It is not so much about simply managing the symptoms – although extreme physiological reactions may require this – but rather about enabling the anxiety states to emerge and, along with them, the experiences that have been denied to awareness in order to protect and preserve the person's self-structure. Anxiety is seen primarily as a product of incongruence. It exists when a person's self-concept as a consistent gestalt is under threat, or in other words, when experiences that have been or are being denied to awareness or distorted in how they are symbolised in awareness (in order to maintain consistency within the person's self-concept) are threatening, or are beginning, to break into awareness.

The necessary and sufficient conditions for constructive personality change that lie at the core of the person-centred approach to therapy refer to the client being in a state of incongruence or anxiety. Working with the presence of anxiety within people therefore becomes a fundamental element within person-centred practice. However, rather than approaching therapy as a means to simply alleviate anxiety, the focus is upon the relational experience that will enable the client's inner process to flow in such a way that constructive personality change can occur. This leads to a more integrated and authentic sense of self as the conditioning of the past is challenged by the new experiences and, within the therapeutic relational climate, allowed to foster a fresh and more realistic sense of self. As this occurs, experiences are accurately symbolised and are included in the self-concept in this accurately symbolised form, and a fuller state of congruence of self and experience develops with a resulting reduction in anxiety.

However, it should be noted that panic and anxiety may not always be rooted in, or the result of, incongruence and threats to the self-structure. Anxiety and panic states can also emerge when a person is in a very congruent state of being, for instance the person who is suddenly facing torture and who knows that he is not going to be able to stop it happening may well experience anxiety and panic and it will have nothing to do with incongruence. Although, having said that, it could be argued that even then an element to the anxiety/panic arises from the fact that the person's psychological belief that such things could never happen to them, or that human beings could never act towards them in that way, could be seen as the breaking down of a denial to awareness. In this example the denial to awareness is towards something that, in this world, is quite possible and does happen – we'd just rather think that it won't happen to us.

Whatever the cause, the reality is that human beings get anxious and at times this reaches a degree of panic. Person-centred therapists do not set themselves up as experts in 'treating' panic and anxiety. Rather, they will regard these as aspects of human nature, elements within the person's internal world that have a role and a place, often developing out of a particular set of experiences and having a particular meaning. Anxiety and panic are to be seen as symptoms, effects, evidence of deeper psychological processes, of conflicts within the person's psychological make-up. Anxiety tells us something about ourselves; it is a kind of warning sign that something is happening, something is moving and shifting within us, some form of psychological conflict or dissonance is threatening to break into awareness.

The following example describes the presence of anxiety in adulthood linked to a developed conditional sense of self founded on childhood experience.

John

John was rarely responded to with love when he cried as a baby and this continued throughout his childhood during which he never felt love from his parents. He couldn't bear to feel that he wasn't loved, so over time he symbolised this experience as being normal and not a judgement upon himself. As an adult he is unable to feel love for others or to receive their love. When he experiences someone who genuinely offers him love he finds this difficult to respond to. It does not match his sense of self as someone who does not experience love. He enters into anxiety states as the new experience threatens and challenges his self-concept and the structure upon which his sense of self has been built.

The person-centred approach both to resolving the inner conflicts that lie behind anxiety and panic and to integrating the effects of this resolution into the totality of awareness of the person is through offering a therapeutically supportive and accepting relational experience. This not only enables and encourages the person to explore their own psychological and emotional landscape but also provides a relational climate in which distortion and conditioning is minimised so that the person can autonomously further develop their self-concept and experience changes within their structure of self that are consistent with new experience.

Other Definitions

Of course, there are different definitions of congruence within person-centred literature, some of which do not involve the notion of 'self-concept'. Where there are a range of meanings presented for congruence, there are difficulties in defining incongruence as well. There are also different views on the nature and content of the self. Mearns and Thorne (2000: 175–6) write of 'edge of awareness' material, elements that are present within the organismic experience but are not present in the person's awareness. They propose an extension of Rogers' notion of the self beyond what is available to the individual's conscious awareness to include such material. When experience is clearly not matching the person's self-structure, and such experience is therefore denied to awareness, it becomes lodged on the edge of the individual's awareness. As it threatens to emerge into awareness, then anxiety becomes the person's response to this process.

Focus on Rogers' Perspective

In this chapter I seek to focus primarily, though not exclusively, on what has become known as Rogers' 'classical' client-centred perspective. Rogers cites the example of a student who might experience an organismic fear of university and of exams, but who rather distorts the experience and creates for himself a belief that his fear is to do with the exams being on the third floor. Hence he creates within himself a defensive belief in relation to heights and stairs to avoid admitting into awareness a sense of his own inadequacy as a student. As Rogers comments, 'to admit a fear of inadequacy would contradict the picture he holds of himself' (Rogers, 1957: 96).

Rogers then continues to develop these ideas by contrasting when a person has no awareness that such incongruence is present with when that person begins dimly to perceive its presence. He indicates that where a person has no awareness of their incongruence then that person is merely vulnerable to the possibility of anxiety and disorganisation of self. In addition, the person will also be vulnerable to experiences occurring so suddenly or so obviously that there is no possibility that any incongruence can be denied. In contrast, if the person dimly perceives incongruence within him- or herself then a tension state develops – this is known as anxiety. Anxiety need not be something sharply perceived by the individual. What is important is that it is experienced as being threatening to the self even though there may not be awareness of the content or nature of the threat. This form of anxiety is often seen in the context of therapy when individuals approach an awareness of some element of their experience that sharply contradicts their self-structure (though not exclusively so).

Symbolisation in Awareness

As incongruence between the concept of self and the total experience of the individual approaches symbolisation in awareness, anxiety is the resulting effect. As this difference or discrepancy becomes more obvious or apparent, any defensive response to threat becomes increasingly difficult to achieve or maintain. Anxiety is therefore seen as the response of the organism to the 'subception' that such discrepancy may enter awareness, which would then force a change in the individual's self-concept (Rogers, 1959: 204). The individual's ability selectively to perceive his or her experiences in terms of the conditions of worth that have come to exist in them becomes unstable and potentially unsustainable.

Self-Structure Under Threat

Another way of describing this process is to say that incongruence can develop when a person's self-structure is felt to be under threat. Anxiety develops and a process of defence occurs, seeking to obstruct the free and accurate experiencing in awareness of the threat.

Jack

Jack was out drinking with his mates when he saw Jill across the room. He could feel a strong attraction and he knew that he wanted to get to know her, but just thinking about going over to her he could feel himself becoming shaky with a cold sweat breaking out. He simply put it down to nerves but the anxiety was enough to make it near impossible for him to make any move. But he was with his mates and he always liked to be seen as confident, it fitted how he thought of himself. He took a deep breath, got up, and headed towards where Jill was standing.

Jack does not really know why he has this reaction. He makes sense of it by putting it down to not being too sure what to say, but in reality deep within his self is a belief that he will be rejected. It is rooted in low self-worth linked to attitudes that he has experienced in the past from significant others that undermined his self-confidence. However, psychologically he cannot afford to allow himself to believe this about himself; it is denied to awareness and this is supported by a general outward portrayal of confidence that is very much part of his self-concept. On the surface he simply knows that he feels anxious, which he puts down to being unsure as to what to say, not aware of the degree of discrepancy that threatens to emerge from within. For some people the discrepancy may simply trigger the symptoms described above, but in other situations where discrepancies threaten they can leave the person experiencing almost a sense of doom. As they seek to undertake some action, or voice some opinion, the element of self that is utterly threatened by what is happening to their sense of self can cause the person to feel as though they are going to die. It can be that strong.

It would be reasonable to suggest that the degree of difference between the person's self-concept and the content of new experience may govern the degree of anxiety that develops. For example, the person who has always believed that they could cope with anything and that their personal will power would always be enough to get them through (because that was what they were always encouraged to believe) now finds that they are losing control of a situation. The threat to their self-concept is such that they would be left feeling utterly undermined. The anxiety response may therefore be extreme, tending towards panic. They may want the kind of help that puts a lid on their symptoms, but this will resolve nothing. The person-centred therapist, by allowing anxiety and panic states to emerge, provides an opportunity for the person to risk acknowledging the existence of the discrepancy or contradiction between their self-structure and the new material entering awareness. This can then be integrated in such a way that there emerges a more complete and consistent, and therefore more congruent, sense of self. Such a sense of self will be more authentic, characterised by a fuller and more accurate range of experience and less modified by conditions of worth and denial to awareness than had previously been the case.

As the anxiety state develops, the client may not at first be aware of what lies behind it. The anxiety is the result of the discrepancy, and the actual nature of that discrepancy may take time to emerge into awareness. Of course, in some instances, it may appear very quickly; the experience of the anxiety and the awareness of the cause may be so closely bound together that they seem impossible to differentiate.

In the following example, a young woman has come into therapy to address a relationship issue and finds anxiety developing in response to the contents of a session. She does not know why at the time. The cause then emerges into her awareness shortly afterwards, but outside of the session.

Maria

Maria is in her early twenties. She has a history of heavy alcohol use associated with sexual disinhibition. She does not know why and it has not been something that she has dwelt on; she has accepted this as being how she is. She likes to think of herself as having autonomy and freedom to be as she wants to be. However, she is troubled that she has been unable to have any lasting relationships and has entered therapy to try and resolve this. The experience of being listened to and accepted makes her feel strangely safe in a way that she has not experienced before. After one particular session she is left feeling significantly anxious. She does not know why but the content of the session related to a period of her early childhood during which she mentioned a male neighbour. It is during that night that she has a vivid dream. It fills her with more intense anxiety as memories of being a target of child sexual abuse break into her awareness.

In response to feeling accepted and understood, some organisimic disquiet has emerged into Maria's awareness. It is not something that she has much experience of and it is not easily symbolised into awareness in a way that is consistent with her self-concept. The memories that then emerge are also 'new' to Maria. She now has to adjust to seeing herself as having been a target of sexual abuse. She also has to engage with the thoughts, feelings and physical reaction to what she now knows about her past, and find a way to symbolise accurately all of this in her awareness. She is no longer the person that she thought she was.

Whether the emergence into awareness of discrepancy and associated anxiety is fast or slow, the person-centred therapist will seek to offer a consistently supportive therapeutic relationship with the client. This relational climate provides encouragement for the client's awareness to be open to more complete and accurate experiencing of the cause of the anxiety. The new material becomes accurately symbolised in the client's awareness, being seen and known more fully. There then follows a process of adjustment as the self-structure adapts in order to come into line with the new experience/information that is no longer denied to awareness. As a result the client begins to move from incongruence to congruence, and this movement is one that Rogers identified as an effect of the person-centred therapeutic conditions and a definite stage of constructive personality change. Indeed, within his seven stages of process Rogers (1967: 148) highlights at Stage 6 that 'the incongruence between experiences and awareness is vividly experienced as it disappears into congruence'.

Emerging Anxiety and Panic in Therapy

Consider the following scenario in which anxiety tending to panic emerges within a therapy session as a result of a mismatch between a client's self-structure and his experience.

Mark

Mark is having counselling at a GP surgery with his counsellor, Annie. Mark likes to be busy in his life. He spends long hours at work; however, he is currently off work, feeling stressed and has been exploring the character traits of his father. He strongly believes that whilst his father was not always there for him, being busy and unavailable due to his work, in reality he was loved by his father. He denies to his experience any real sense of loss or that, perhaps, his father saw his work as more important to him than his son. Such an idea would be too disturbing to accept, and would threaten the picture that he has had to construct of himself as being a son that was loved by his father; it was just that his father had an important career and had to provide for the family.

At some deep level, however, outside of Mark's awareness, there is present within his organismic experience a sense of despair at his father's unavailability, and a desire never to be like that to his own children. Physiological symptoms of anxiety emerge into the client's awareness within the therapy session, but he is not making conscious connections in his awareness as to the cause. He knows something isn't right within himself but cannot identify what it is. Mark finds himself feeling strange; the therapist picks up on it and acknowledges that he seems to look worried and distant. Material outside of his awareness is making an impact. He cannot define it in his awareness; however, its presence is inducing a sense of unease, disturbance, symptoms of emerging anxiety. His concept of self is under threat.

The counsellor empathises, acknowledging in a slightly questioning tone her sense of his seeming unsettled. It allows Mark to distinguish more clearly the disturbing nature of what he is experiencing and it leaves him feeling shaky. He experiences physical symptoms, heaviness in his arms and a tingling, slightly spaced-out numbness.

(Continued)

(Continued)

Mark's focus is still with the effects of the emerging threat to his self-structure. He is not engaging with the cause – this remains out of awareness. A cold sweat breaks out as an insight breaks into his awareness. He simply says 'Oh shit!' and goes quiet. His therapist empathises, speaking gently and waits. Mark has suddenly made connections between himself and his father, seeing his own tendency towards always needing to be busy as being just like his father. It is shocking and is followed by another thought but this is too threatening to Mark's sense of self to be able to accept or voice. It is that not only was his father not there for him, but also that he, in turn is not being there for his own children. The sense of his father as having not been there for him now rushes upon him, profoundly disrupting his self-concept as someone who was loved by his father, and who himself is there for his own children.

The counsellor empathises, it holds him on his insight. Anxiety rises again as another thought develops. He keeps it to himself. It is too painful to verbalise. Had he ever really felt loved by his father? And, as he now suspects that he hadn't, maybe his father had never really loved him.

Anxiety verging on panic is likely to be the symptom of this inner process of realisation. A key aspect of the client's self-structure is breaking down and being reorganised. The person-centred therapist will need to be very focused, clearly conveying the unconditional positive regard that she is experiencing for her client, maintaining simple yet accurate empathy, and at the same time maintaining her own congruent state. Where a client's incongruence rises to the surface it is vital that the counsellor does not lose her own congruence. Her full and open presence is needed to offer a supportive and reliable presence for the client, who may be psychologically in pieces.

It may take time for the insight described in the scenario above to be absorbed, allowing Mark's self-structure to adjust to the new insight. However, there will be situations in which the implications cannot be easily absorbed. The insight can be so shattering that the client cannot cope with the tension that arises. They may find themselves confused, not knowing who they are, particularly if they have invested a great deal of their sense of self in the aspect of their self-concept that is now so clearly under threat. More anxiety can arise and it could develop into a panic attack, the client unable to hold the conflict within themselves. Where this arises the client may be hyperventilating or struggling to breathe. The therapist needs to remain calm and reach through the panic reactions to the client, seeking to maintain contact, offer reassurance and help him to feel supported.

Anxiety or panic attacks can be very frightening and debilitating, and they can occur within counselling sessions, particularly where something shocking or overwhelming occurs for the client. In the above example, Mark has been shocked. Insight has broken into his awareness, not only threatening his belief that he is different to his father in terms of his character traits, but also threatening his self-structure as a man loved by his father. He may feel ready to explore this now; he may not, preferring to use time in the session to regain some degree of composure and integration.

From a person-centred perspective it is important to trust the client to know what is right for them. The client will, however, be feeling very vulnerable and will benefit therapeutically from the counsellor's communicated unconditional positive regard and readiness to convey empathic understanding. Both of these attitudinal qualities will emerge from the counsellor's congruent presence within the therapeutic relationship. This will allow and support the client to make their *own* sense of what they have experienced and to attach their *own* meaning to it, and, from this, adjustments will occur within their sense or structure of self.

Throughout the above, the person-centred practitioner does not attempt to make sense of the experience. She may help him to control the physiological reactions, for instance if a panic attack affects his breathing, but otherwise she allows him to be as he needs to be, as the anxiety and then panic arises and as material breaks into his awareness. What can now be expected from this session is that Mark, feeling encouraged by the therapeutic relationship with the counsellor, will begin to process what is now present in his awareness.

Of course, this whole process raises the question as to whether, as material emerges into awareness, the therapeutic focus should be on the anxiety reactions associated with the new material, or the material itself. One client may place more focus on the anxiety reaction, another on the insights that are breaking into awareness. In practice there is often movement between the two. The person-centred therapist needs to be sensitive and responsive, moving with the client and holding an attitude of acceptance that within the client's self is a knowing of what is needed. The therapist can only respond to that which the client communicates; to do otherwise would be directive and unacceptable within the principles of person-centred practice.

Working with clients for whom material is emerging into awareness can make the client feel worse before they feel better. A client can experience increased anxiety and interpret this as meaning that the counselling is making them more anxious and is therefore unhelpful. In extreme cases a client may withdraw from counselling for this reason. What is actually occurring is that the client is simply becoming more aware of the level of anxiety that they have, in other words, becoming more sensitive to the degree of incongruence that is present within them. There will be times when the counsellor may offer this insight to reassure the client.

Psychological Breakdown and Disorganisation

Rogers (1959: 228–9) also wrote of the process of psychological breakdown and disorganisation. He described four stages to this process, the first two stages of which 'may be illustrated by anxiety-producing experiences in therapy, or by acute psychotic breakdowns'.

1   If the individual has a large or significant degree of *incongruence between self and experience* and if a significant experience demonstrating this *incongruence* occurs suddenly, or with a high degree of obviousness, then the organism's process of *defense* is unable to operate successfully.

2   As a result *anxiety is experienced*, as the *incongruence* is subceived. The degree of anxiety is dependent upon the extent of the *self-structure* which is *threatened*.

Rogers then went on to describe the effects that this has on the individual's self-structure and subsequent behaviour. He writes:

3   The process of defense being unsuccessful, the *experience* is *accurately symbolized* in *awareness*, and the gestalt of the *self-structure* is broken by this *experience* of the *incongruence* in *awareness*. A state of disorganization results.

4   In such a state of disorganization the organism behaves at times in ways which are openly consistent with experiences which have hitherto been distorted or denied to awareness. At other times the self may temporarily regain regnancy and the organism may behave in ways consistent with it. Thus in such a state of disorganization, the tension between the concept of self (with its included distorted perceptions), and the experiences which are not accurately symbolized or included in the concept of self, is expressed in a confused regnancy, first one and then the other supplying the 'feedback' by which the organism regulates behavior.

So, denied material breaking into awareness disrupts the individual's self and in extreme cases can shatter it, leading to psychotic breakdown. Within this process anxiety states emerge that, as the threat to the self-concept increases, can induce states more akin to panic and in extreme cases what is often grouped under the term 'psychosis'.

Anxiety, Panic and Terror in Response to Traumatising Experience

Another process that can lead to the existence of anxiety and panic is where a person has been subjected to an intense and damaging relational experience that has left them with a self-image that has developed specifically in response to what they have experienced. This could be seen as simply an element within the self-structure or, as has been suggested by Mearns and Thorne (2000: 102), as a 'configuration of self'. Another way to think of this is as being an area of woundedness and sensitivity within the self-structure that, when approached, releases a set of feelings that were linked with its creation as well as the anxiety associated with it threatening to engulf the individual with painful experiencing. Whilst in some cases an element of that area of self may be in discrepancy with the person's self-structure, this is not the case in the scenario below.

Angela I

Angela's structure of self has been affected as a result of being subject to domestic violence over a number of years. For her, verbal and physical violence has created low self-esteem that is associated with feelings of anxiety, panic and terror induced through her traumatising experiences. Angela had not found it easy coming to counselling. She had not long left her partner of ten years. He had been physically and verbally violent towards her. She knew that she had somehow to put the past behind her, but how? It never seemed to go away. And she was anxious about so many things. Anything sudden and unexpected, a noise, a sudden movement from someone physically close to her and she would jump and it would take her ages to calm down from the experience. She wasn't sure if she knew what 'calm' meant anymore.

It is her tenth counselling session. She has talked a bit about her past, but mostly about her life now and the challenges she faces on a day-to-day basis. She finds it hard to go out and her confidence is very low. Things had begun to improve but have now got worse following her ex-partner phoning her after a break in their contact. He doesn't know where she lives, but he does have her phone number. The call was so that they could arrange for him to see their daughter.

Angela found that hearing his voice, the swearing, putting her down, always putting her down, made her feel so small, so useless, wanting to hide in the corner like a terrified mouse. It always leaves her shaking. In the counselling session she has so many memories surfacing, the sounds, the feelings of terror, the beatings. She feels her anxiety rising. It is hard for her to speak; her speech is broken up by the short breaths that are all she can take.

The person-centred therapist role is to be there with and for Angela, ensuring that he is communicating the therapeutic conditions and offering a genuinely human response to a person in pain, terror and distress.

Angela II

Angela's counsellor, Gerry, empathises with the awfulness that Angela is experiencing of having her ex-partner in her head; he offers in his tone of voice a genuinely human response to a person in pain and distress.

Angela feels heard by Gerry's response and there is something reassuring about that, yet she finds her anxiety rising and there is more, as though she is engulfed in sensations that are too much to think about. It is as though there is something else but she does not have a sense of what that something else is. She does not speak; she does not have words for what she is experiencing.

Whether or not there is verbal communication occurring, the counsellor will maintain their attitudinal qualities towards the client, working to ensure that their presence is reflecting the relational qualities of congruence, empathy and unconditional positive regard. As the client communicates what she is experiencing, the counsellor will be openly responsive and yet also consistently present as a companion on the client's inner journey.

Angela III

Terror breaks through. It is as though an area of her self that has stored so many painful feelings has burst open. It is not a new experience but when she is engulfed by it she wishes that she was dead. Angela voices this, her speech still broken by the short breaths that she is having to take. She says that she can't stop it when it takes over like this and blames herself for letting herself become how she is. Yet she also acknowledges that she couldn't do anything about it and Gerry empathises with this view and speaks with a profound sense of compassion. To Angela it seems as though Gerry understands. That sense of being understood allows her to feel somehow safer in herself. She feels strangely less threatened by what she is feeling.

Therapeutic response is, of course, not simply what you say, but how you say it. The person-centred counsellor will wish to be congruent in his communication, allowing what he feels to affect the tone of what he is communicating. Gerry's experience was one of compassion – how is compassion different from unconditional positive regard? Perhaps compassion is a facet of unconditional positive regard, or vice versa. However, what is vital is that whatever feelings of compassion and caring are communicated in these situations, they have to be genuinely heartfelt. Acceptance and unconditional positive regard are not a cognitive, head-centred process. To be therapeutically significant, unconditional positive regard has to be experienced viscerally by the counsellor.

In the above example, an area of terror from within Angela has emerged into the therapeutic relationship. This is not something new to Angela. This is all too familiar to her. She knows that what she experiences seems to be a precursor to its emergence. But she also knows that when it emerges it takes over, dominating her experience of herself.

Years of violence – physical and verbal – have taken their toll. The anxiety reactions have established themselves within Angela's structure of self, not only the anxiety but other thoughts, feelings and behaviours that, time and again, have been induced by her experience as a target of violence. These are not 'edge of awareness' experiences as demonstrated in Mark's scenario. These are experiences that are well known to the client, elements of herself of which she has had awareness for some while. But feeling able to voice what she is experiencing, and feeling heard and understood, leaves her feeling strangely safer. Changes are taking place within her structure of self. She does not have to fight her feelings; they are being accepted, and maybe she can accept them in a different kind of way. The anxiety reduces a little.

Integrating Painful Areas of Self

In the above example, the challenge in therapy is less about coming to terms with something new, something threatening to the person's self-structure. Rather therapy becomes a matter of enabling the anxiety- and terror-driven areas of the client's structure of self to be heard, genuinely accepted and understood. And not just by the counsellor. The therapeutic process is likely to involve the client establishing a new relationship with this area of herself so that there may be the possibility of greater integration. The client may need to be able to offer unconditional positive self-regard at an intra-personal level towards the anxious and terrified parts of herself. To do this, though, means experiencing their presence, and often what is happening is that the client is seeking to push such painful experiences away, hence the difficulty in establishing unconditional positive self-regard.

A constructive outcome could be that the client is able to redefine her concept of self by gradually freeing herself from feelings of vulnerability and beliefs about herself that resulted from the violence and the undermining of her self-worth. Sometimes, however, the psychological wounds never fully heal and there is always a psychological sensitivity to particular areas of experiencing.

In some instances, the area or part may have developed to the degree that it has such a strong identity (configuration of self or dissociated state) for it to literally have its own voice; the counsellor may then find themselves speaking directly to it. If this occurs, this 'aspect of self' must be offered the same therapeutic conditions. The therapist is likely to have to respond not only to the anxiety and panic locked within this part or area of self, but also the anxiety that the client feels towards that area of her self.

Repelling the Threat to Self

In the examples of Mark and Angela there has been an openness to the experiencing that is emerging into their awareness, even though it is, if you like, occurring through two different psychological processes. However, for some clients the sense of anxiety may be too much. The threat, even if not consciously known, may be sensed to be too potentially overwhelming or they may feel that the therapy is simply making them worse, and they wish to try to restore the 'normality' that was their previous experiencing.

The client who seeks to repel the threat, to push back the material that is emerging, or to distort its meaning in order to maintain their self-structure, may well succeed. But it is likely that the material will seek to re-emerge at some other time. A behavioural response, if it has not already occurred, is that the client may resort to other means to repel the experiences that are touching into their awareness, for instance through the use of alcohol or other substances, or maybe through obsessive behaviours that can absorb them in order to create a psychological barrier to what is seeking to emerge. Where this occurs, the person-centred therapist will be offering unconditional acceptance of the client's choices. Often, the very fact that they experience acceptance of how they need to be can enable the client to self-question. The person-centred response is not a technique to achieve this but it can be the result that occurs as a result of the client experiencing the therapeutic conditions. People can begin to take the risk of questioning their coping strategies if they are experiencing a climate of therapeutic relationship, and to risk, therefore, the emergence into awareness of the material being denied, obstructed or obscured.

The Congruence Continuum

In person-centred theory, the human condition is naturally one of integration, and the actualising tendency that Rogers defined tends to integrate rather than fragment although it may need the therapeutic relationship, or a relationship having similar quality and tone outside of the therapy room, to facilitate this. Rogers wrote of the notion that the person moves from a state of fixity to fluidity, and this would suggest that for fluidity to occur then there would need to be an increasing absence of obstructing elements seeking to separate or hinder that flow. He also described (1967: 157) the process of movement from incongruence to congruence as a continuum. At one end of the continuum is a maximum degree of incongruence that is quite unknown to the person. There are then stages in which the contradictions and discrepancies within the person are subject to increasingly sharp recognition leading to the experiencing of incongruence in the immediate present, with more accurate symbolising in awareness leading to its dissipation. The other end of the continuum is characterised by little more than temporary incongruence between experiencing and awareness. Here, the individual would not need to defend himself against the threatening aspects of his experience.

Conclusion

Anxiety and panic states can develop as a result of incongruence and discrepancy between the individual's picture of themselves and the content of experience within their structure of self. This discrepancy may be known or unknown to the person. However, it is often unknown and the experiences associated with it have been symbolised in awareness in a distorting manner, generally in order to maintain a particular self-structure. Anxiety and panic are natural reactions and prompts to process this.

Anxiety and panic states can also be held within the structure of self. These may be thought of as 'configurations of self' or as wounded areas of increased sensitivity that are painful to approach. However we think of them, they can emerge strongly, bringing anxiety and panic states into the reality of a person's experience and awareness. They can (although they do not always) originate from some form of traumatic experiencing. In extreme cases (see Kirshen Rundle's chapter on 'Person-Centred Approaches to Different Realities' in this book), dissociative states can develop, generally as a result of traumatic experiencing in early life. Again, these can contain associated anxiety and panic or, as the memories are recovered, can bring profound anxiety to the person, who is faced with the horror of what they had experienced but which had been dissociated from their normal, everyday awareness.

Person-centred therapy enables the individual to become more aware of incongruence and to move towards greater congruence and thus 'a more authentic sense of self'. The principles and attitudinal values of the person-centred approach, and the emphasis placed on the therapeutic relationship, are key to helping people create greater authenticity both in themselves and in their lives. As a result, this can enable them to lead a fuller and more satisfying human experience.

Rogers (1967: 187–8) suggests that through the therapeutic experience the client develops 'an increasing openness to experience', and suggests that if a person could be fully open to his or her experience then every stimulus (be it originating from within the organism or in the external environment) could then be 'freely relayed through the nervous system without being distorted by any defensive mechanism'. In such a genuinely open state, one in which experience flows naturally and fully into awareness, we would perhaps see the fulfilment of the person as a living process. Then, the presence of anxiety or panic might be regarded not as a defensive reaction to some inner process linked to the presence of incongruence, but as something that occurs as a natural and normal reaction of a fully aware person to a situation or event carrying a degree of threat and uncertainty that demands such experiencing.

I have no doubt that the person-centred approach, both in terms of theory and practice, offers a great deal to explain the development of anxiety and panic states. It shows how the day-to-day sense of self so ably strives to protect itself from 'threatening to self' material that underlies the incongruencies and discrepancies between experience and awareness. And, perhaps more importantly, it describes the therapeutic process that can help to resolve them.

Guide to Further Reading

Because anxiety can be associated with so many client experiences, and is a product of incongruence, almost any book, chapter or paper dealing with a person-centred approach to a specific client, group of clients or client experience is likely to be relevant to understanding the experience of anxiety per se and therefore of panic. Each of the works listed in the reference section here and in the other chapters would play some part in expanding your knowledge. The following other three references are listed below.

Bryant-Jefferies, R. (2005) *Counselling Victims of Warfare*. Abingdon: Radcliffe Press.

This provides an explanation of person-centred counselling processes linked to the impact of traumatic experiences on the person.

Bryant-Jefferies, R. (2005) *Counselling a Survivor of Childhood Sexual Abuse*. Abingdon: Radcliffe Press.

This book provides an explanation of person-centred counselling processes linked to the memories emerging into awareness, associated anxiety and the impact on self.

Warner, M.S. (2000) 'Person-centred therapy at the difficult edge: A developmentally based model of fragile and dissociated process', in D. Mearns and B. Thorne (eds), *Person-Centred Therapy Today: New Frontiers in Theory and Practice.* London: Sage, pp. 144–71.

This addresses areas where anxiety and panic can often be a feature of the client's experience.

References

Mearns, D. and Thorne, B. (eds) (2000) *Person-Centred Therapy Today: New Frontiers in Theory and Practice*. London: Sage.

Rogers, C.R. (1957) 'The necessary and sufficient conditions of therapeutic personality change', *Journal of Consulting Psychology*, 21: 95–103.

Rogers, C.R. (1959) 'A theory of therapy, personality and interpersonal relationships as developed in the client-centred framework', in S. Koch (ed.), *Psychology: A Study of a Science*, Vol. 3. *Formulations of the Person and the Social Context*. New York: McGraw-Hill, pp. 184–256.

Rogers, C.R. (1967) *On Becoming a Person*. London: Constable.

7

PERSON-CENTRED APPROACHES TO DIFFERENT REALITIES

KIRSHEN RUNDLE

Though this be madness, yet there is method in't.

(Hamlet, II.ii, 205–6)

The Problem of Therapy with Clients who Experience Different Realities

Counsellors can feel disconcerted when confronted with an unusual way of being or a description of a client as mentally ill. How do we work with a person who can hear voices, with a person in a state of disintegration whose speech is florid or difficult to track? Is something extra or different required of us? It can be difficult to trust the necessity and sufficiency of the therapeutic conditions if we are unsettled by a client's strange behaviour. So it is tempting to take refuge in medical diagnoses hoping that they will help us understand client behaviour as symptoms of a 'disorder' or 'illness'. Reliance on these fixed-state labels may lead us to believe that we are more likely to offer the 'correct treatment' for a particular problem.

But how does that fit with the person-centred approach that unconditionally values client uniqueness, trusts clients as the experts in what hurts and what helps, and accepts clients' current experiencing as their reality?

Taking a Person-Centred Approach

Rogers' theory of personality (1959) and his nineteen propositions (1951) suggest that the need to make sense of experience is so strong that human beings will try, in any way possible, to process it. Our theoretical need for valuing and acceptance also means that we try especially hard to make sense of those relationships most important to us. Conditions of worth arise as we deny and distort those experiences that are at odds with our pictures of how we think we should be. When the incongruence between our experience and our view of ourselves becomes too great, we can no longer hold onto our sense of ourselves and, for some people, this leads to a chaotic disintegration of their lives.

If we accept Rogers' view that we are all subject to some level of psychological maladjustment or disorganisation (Rogers, 1959: 228) and his notion of the self as a process of becoming rather than as a fixed entity, we can see that all behaviours, feelings, ways of being fall along continua. Then, when do levels of distress or eccentricity become symptomatic of 'mental illness' such as those called depression, schizophrenia, or anxiety, bipolar and personality disorders? We can all act, feel, think in ways that do not make sense to us – let alone others. Falling in love can be a very good example of delusional behaviour and an odd reality but, it is not classified as 'mental illness'! I suggest that perceptions of madness or altered reality are more to do with a lack of conformity to the social and cultural norms of the person making the judgements. Specifically, some people seem especially vulnerable in current Western culture where personal freedom and autonomy are valued, and a meaningful sense of self and the ability to be self-reliant are required.

Making Sense of Different Realities in a Person-Centred Way

Rather than imposing rigid, potentially stigmatising, diagnoses of mental illness that characterise the whole person, Margaret Warner (2000, 2006, 2007) proposes that unusual ways of being can be accounted for in 'difficult process' terms, which can overlap and may not be present in every situation (Warner, 2000: 145). Warner's position is that 'difficult process' results when early childhood difficulties mean important processing capabilities are not developed (ibid.). She suggests that a person-centred way of understanding and working with these clients can support them in their difficulties with processing, and helps nurture more well-developed capacities over time. Examples include the following.

Fragile process: When early important relationships are perceived to be inconsistent or lacking in empathy, it is difficult to build a sense of self that is reliable. Experiences tend to be held in attention at very low, or very high, levels of intensity. When it is difficult to hold onto, or trust, one's own experiencing to such a great degree, it is even more difficult to assimilate others' points of view without feeling the threat of annihilation. Careful listening and precise reflection are critical with people suffering fragile process, as any misunderstanding can be seen as threatening to their control over their lives. At an extreme level people are unable to engage with others for any length of time and may come to feel that they are under attack emotionally or even physically. (See Matt below.)

Dissociated process: Severe childhood trauma can lead to a defence of dissociation where different aspects of self are regarded, or referred to, as different people. In this way the traumatic experience can be kept at a distance and does not have to be integrated into one's sense of self. (See Kayleigh below.) These dissociated parts can, at times, alter a client's perceptions such that it is as if some other person is present and experiencing what is happening (Warner, 2000: 162).

Psychotic process: The ways that people with this style of processing make sense of their experiencing tends not to make sense for others within their cultures. This means that there is little likelihood of their reality offering 'predictive validity in relation to their environment' (Warner, 2006: 13). This will impair their abilities to relate to others effectively and, especially when coupled with experiences of hearing voices, hallucinations or delusions, can lead to awareness of difference, not being understood and then isolation. (See Joan and Ruby below.)

Metaphact process: Warner's view is that some people have an idiosyncratic way of understanding, interpreting and coming to conclusions about the way that things are. She suggests that this style of processing creates a hybrid form of communication from combining ordinary facts with metaphors, especially when a person is struggling to make sense of complex, unusual or emotional experiences (Warner, 2007: 143-4). At times this imposes a peculiarly literal and factual perspective onto what would be seen by others to be quite clearly a figure of speech or metaphor. As she points out, sign language can appear odd and incomprehensible to those with no knowledge of it. But, once understood, all becomes clear. If the therapist can find a way to understand this language rather than expecting the client to engage in hers, then a deep mutual understanding can be reached. (See Devendra below.)

Initially, I was wary that these are also generic labels that go against a fundamental person-centred premise – the uniqueness of the individual. Margaret Warner has said, however, that she intends such descriptors to be an aid to understanding that can free the therapist up to be more empathic. If they get in the way of empathy then the therapist would be better advised to dispense with them (Warner, personal communication, 2008).

The Process of Helping People Make Sense of their Worlds

Rogers suggests that the process of therapy follows seven stages (Rogers, 1961: 125–59). As clients progress they change from seeing themselves as objects and separate, towards accepting themselves as people and integrating aspects of self. It is rare for clients to go through all seven stages during therapy, most tending to move between three or four of the middle stages, at their own pace, even moving backwards at times.

The following example shows how Matt did move through all seven stages of process – though some of the movement took place after he had ended his therapy.

Matt I

Matt had always considered himself to be a successful person, leading a happy, settled life. He had three younger sisters and a close extended family, and he played cricket to a high level. But, when he was eighteen, his mother left his father and he found himself in crisis. He began to drink so heavily the night before a cricket match that he was unable to play well and lost his place in the team. He took so many days off work that he lost his job and his parents were shocked and disappointed with him. He was sent to prison after setting fire to a new sofa in the house and became aggressive and disruptive, often setting fires in his cell or flooding it. Staff and other prisoners regarded him as a 'nutter' and kept away from him. He talked of hearing voices, said that people were taking his things, putting disgusting things in his food, infecting his cell. Eventually, he was diagnosed with borderline personality disorder and schizophrenia.

After vandalising a pool table, verbally abusing an officer, then flooding his cell, Matt was told that he must start therapy. He said that this was a waste of time, it was for losers and he was strong. Also that it wouldn't change anything as it was other people who made him behave violently. When I met him, he laughed at what he called his 'naughty' behaviour and took great delight in telling me that he was mentally ill so what he did was not his fault anyway. He said that his offence and disruptive behaviour were caused by his illness. He was also quite clear that he wanted to be left alone and didn't need company or friendship as 'you can only rely on yourself anyway and people always let you down'. He revelled in his reputation as a hard, aggressive man.

As is common at Stage 1 of the seven stages of processing, Matt had not voluntarily come into therapy. He was unwilling or unable to communicate self, and it appeared that internal communication was blocked as he neither recognised nor owned his feelings. He felt threatened by close communicative relationships, and was emphatic that he had no problems and so he had no desire to change.

Matt II

Nevertheless, Matt always attended his sessions as arranged, was unfailingly polite and even cleaned the room before I arrived. He said that it was because I treated him with respect. Our initial sessions were characterised by his inability to follow any train of thought. I struggled to track him. Sometimes it felt as if he wasn't even aware that I was in the room. When I reflected back what he said he would contradict immediately himself or question whether it was acceptable for him to think that way. If I offered a cautious paraphrasing it was as if he took it as a new way of thinking that he should accept as the right way. At times he was not in psychological contact with me (the first of Rogers' (1959) therapeutic conditions). Then, as Prouty suggests in his pre-therapy work (Prouty et al., 2002), concrete reflections of what was happening with us both, such as saying that he was smiling, or looking out of the window or had said my name, would bring him back and he could resume our discussion. Still, however, he constantly stressed that he was strong, happy and successful. He talked of his family and his childhood but could not describe his feelings, merely explaining things as 'just the way I am' or 'the way I was brought up'.

Supervision was critical in helping me resist the temptation to try and move Matt along. I found it hard to remain patient and really to trust that Matt knew best when he seemed to be asking me to give him the answers and when there seemed to be no movement.

Here (Stage 2), Matt's experience of being 'received' by me encouraged a loosening of expression. He sometimes talked easily about non-self topics but presented as facts his rigid and unrecognised personal constructs. He still saw problems as external to himself and accepted no responsibility for them. Feelings, personal meanings and experience were remote and not owned and he did not recognise his constant contradictions.

Matt III

After a few weeks he told me that he had been sexually assaulted at the age of six. His parents had told him that he would be fine as he was 'a strong boy', but he was confused because his overwhelming feelings of fear, distress and uncertainty didn't match this picture. This was the first time that he expressed distress to me and he talked of the voices that still tormented him about it happening again. We spent several sessions exploring this trauma and then one week he mentioned the breakup of his parents' marriage. That was when I made a big mistake. I was so pleased that he had told me of some feelings and of two difficult experiences that I asked him what it was like for him to be confronted with a different picture of his family life. That crossed the line from encounter into invasion (Mearns and Cooper, 2005: 103) and he defended himself by blocking me. He responded that it was

(Continued)

(Continued)

fine, he could handle it, and it was up to them. He had started to be able to trust and receive my empathy and I had taken advantage of him.

I was worried that I had undone all the progress we had made towards building a reliable relationship that went at his pace. So I apologised the following week and he smiled, saying that there was no need. Somehow that caused a big shift in our relationship and he talked of feeling angry that the voices were trying to keep him in the past, reminding him of something that he should have got over by now. That was the first acknowledgement of his feeling something in the present and it was as if my apology had convinced him that I was genuine enough to trust with further discussion of the traumatic assault.

Most of Matt's work at this time was at Stage 3. He could talk of his past trauma and reflected on the feelings and personal meanings about it. But he could not do the same with experiences or feelings that were not so remote. He came to recognise that there were contradictions between his feelings and his constructs. But he still found it difficult to accept those feelings as other than shameful, bad or abnormal. The session where I apologised marked a quite dramatic shift into Stage 4, though he sometimes seemed to move backwards to other stages.

Matt IV

At times we had a session when he would be scattered or not want to talk to me, and he still occasionally had fights with other prisoners. But he had stopped flooding or setting fires in his cell. Whilst isolation can be threatening to the sense of self, the opportunity to re-engage or to engage differently can feel equally threatening, as can the opportunity to become open to the flow of one's experiencing or to explore the development of a revised self-structure. It seemed that he sometimes got frightened at the changes and had to take refuge in his previous way of being for a while.

It was a very slow process but, by staying exactly where he was each week, by reflecting his words, and by accepting, without denying its reality, the chaos that was going on for him, he was eventually able to feel safe enough to be open to what he was feeling and to look at what it meant. When the acknowledgement of those feelings didn't make things worse, he became less scared of what was actually going on for him and more prepared to look at which aspects of his previous self-structure felt 'as if they belonged' to him. Once he had done this he was able to admit to his anger at his parents for not helping him deal with the childhood trauma, for splitting up, for 'making a lie' of his childhood. He was terribly sad about all those things but felt that he really did have an inner strength that would help him make a happy life for himself.

At Stage 4 Matt still regarded a close relationship as dangerous but began to risk relating on a feeling basis. He easily described more intense feelings from the past, and could sometimes express his current experiencing with, tentatively, the feelings that accompanied it. He came to recognise and question contradictions and incongruities in his self-concept, as well as experiencing some sense of personal responsibility for his current problems and choices.

Matt V

After about four months Matt was able to look at his fear, disgust and shame about having been raped, and accept those feelings as valid without seeing them as a reflection of any weakness in him. He managed to separate himself as he is today from the little boy and realise that he now had the capacity to deal differently with problems in his life. At this stage the voices suddenly stopped. He said that it was as if this person was not under threat – he now felt that the voices, distressing as they were, had acted as a warning to be careful rather than as a reminder that his weakness would lead to a repeat of it.

He started to feel remorse for the disruption that he had caused in the prison and no longer needed to play 'the hard man'. He could see the value in having close relationships, even if they might go wrong. Being prepared to take the risk of trusting people and allowing himself to be vulnerable with them was the biggest shift at this time. He was very clear that his family needed to accept the man he really was rather than the idealised version that they had tried to impose on him. He also came to believe that, when bad things happened in his life, he would feel unhappy or angry but that 'life is like that sometimes and grown-ups have to deal with it'.

Matt's process at this time is indicative of Stage 5. He was much closer to his organismic being and to the flow of his feelings. Despite his fear and mistrust he increasingly expressed and owned his feelings freely, as in the present. He critically examined personal constructs, meanings and incongruities and expressed a desire to be, and be seen as, 'the real me'. Alongside this came an increasing recognition of personal responsibility and choice.

Matt VI

Towards the end of his sentence Matt was moved to a secure unit and our counselling stopped. He continued to receive therapeutic support there to help him plan for life after his release.

During this time he came to regard his offence as a desperate attempt to impose some sort of order on his life that was spiralling out of control, rather than something to do with a 'psychotic episode'. He discussed his losses and anguish without reliving them so painfully and was more able to talk of what he felt in that moment.

(Continued)

(Continued)

Forgiving his parents for failing to help him deal with the childhood assault seemed to be a key moment of release for him. He said that he was aware of what might cause struggles in the future and how he would cope. He no longer felt the pressure of trying to live up to the idealised version of himself that he had grown up with, and he could listen to his own voice and experiencing.

Stage 6 is crucial and often indicative of lasting change. Matt could accept fully both immediacy of feeling and the feeling itself – even when difficult. He was *living* his experience as a process, not feeling *about* it. Self and problems as objects or 'out there' became what was felt and lived subjectively. He felt free from former structures and constructs so that he could differentiate his experiencing sharply.

Matt VII

Even though he has been released Matt still turns up at the secure unit occasionally. When he needs more than his own inner resilience, he feels it offers a place where he is accepted without any pressure to live in a certain way. Once he has gathered his resources about him again he is able to return to the world with all its stresses and strains. He is taking responsibility for his actualising process in a very concrete and practical way. He knows and accepts himself, can feel when he is starting to lose himself and has found a way of dealing with it that maintains and enhances his way of being.

Clients often decide that they no longer need therapy by Stage 7. For Matt, he trusts his process and owns his changing feelings, experiencing situations in a subjective way. He tentatively holds personal constructs that he tests against his experience and adapts accordingly. His internal communication is clear and he is aware of his sense of self and the choices that he has in this new way of being.

The conditions of worth that Matt had developed were so powerful that he had come to believe that he was living a charmed existence. He was told that he was successful, strong and able to cope in all he did; any actual failures and trauma were reinterpreted or dismissed; suspicion that his family were anything other than idyllically happy was denied. When his family broke up, however, his feelings were so intense, and so at odds with his picture of himself, that he did not know how to cope. The denials and distortions that had served as defences were no longer enough to protect him. It is, perhaps, no surprise that being plunged into such a vulnerable state would enable the resurfacing of distress around an unresolved trauma.

When this is coupled with a style of processing that has never had the chance to develop its own voice, the result is an external locus of evaluation and a fragmented sense of self.

My empathic responding in a non-directive way helped him begin to be open to the flow of his experiencing, however scattered it may initially have been. Genuine, unconditional acceptance of people in a vulnerable state offers a major therapeutic benefit when the response to any sign of 'weakness' in the past has been rejection or denial of the reality of feelings. When people are in such a fragmented state, fulfilment of Rogers' sixth condition – that the communication of the therapist conditions is achieved – is hindered because people's own experiences are incomprehensible to them and their experience of other people has been inconsistent or untrustworthy.

Listening to the Music Behind the Words

Communication of empathic understanding fosters the development of trust, reconnection with others and the ability then to look at one's experiencing in a different way. Empathic responding and unconditional acceptance help a client to feel heard (maybe for the first time) but do not require therapists to accept that something is true when we know that it is not. Congruent self-awareness enables us to empathise without colluding and helps us to understand the meaning of (seemingly) bizarre experiences for each individual. We must be clear about what is different for us and acknowledge that to the client. This 'as if' element of empathy is also important in demonstrating to the client that to be separate does not have to be threatening or isolating. Trust in the consistency of the genuine, accepting and empathic (but separate) counsellor acts as an anchor that enables a scared or vulnerable client to feel safe enough to risk exploring issues that may never have been addressed before. Even clients who are scared at losing touch with reality or who feel that they are 'going mad' may, ultimately, feel able to reflect differently on the denials, distortions and conditions of worth that have led to their tenuous connection to the world being threatened.

When it Goes Wrong ...

When a client's sense of self is disintegrating or fragmenting and normal defences become inadequate, barriers to understanding and relating are further reinforced. Empathic understanding of a personal metaphor or code and the communication of this understanding to the client are then the only way to penetrate those barriers. The therapist must accept the reality of the unusual experience – as it is for the client – without changing it, denying its existence or keeping distant from it. Any reflections, paraphrasing or challenges must be grounded in what is actually said but it is also important to listen for clues to discover the idiosyncratic meaning. Misunderstandings, incorrect assumptions or denials confirm a client's sense of being un-understandable so that no further risk at communicating is taken. This happened in the example below.

Devendra

Devendra had enjoyed his intellectual experience at university but never really seemed to fit in with his peers. At first, his unusual dress sense had drawn people to him and it had felt good that his individuality was – for the first time – appreciated. But, as time went on, he just didn't seem able to hold onto, or develop, close friendships where people cared as much as he did about talking in the ways that he liked to talk about things. Successive disappointments had led to his withdrawing into his own world – just as he had done when at school. He tried to be kind and lively as he saw other students being but his words or actions were invariably misunderstood – seemed almost to frighten those he wanted to make friends with. He tried hard not to mind and see it as their problem or as an expression of racism but it didn't always work.

He was unable to find a job on graduating so he moved back with his parents. After two years, however, they were becoming increasingly worried about him. He was lethargic, he hardly bothered to wash or to take care of himself and he rarely appeared to have contact with people apart from them.

At our initial session he was lively and engaging. He told me that he spent most of his time alone and seemed really to enjoy having the chance to talk with someone. He was wearing an odd combination of clothes but I just thought it was endearing that he didn't mind about convention. His topics of conversation were eccentric too but, again, I interpreted it as an idiosyncratic take on the world. As he laughed at my misunderstandings I relaxed and assumed the 'real' work would come later, when he had settled into the therapeutic relationship.

I was astounded when his mother called later to say that Devendra had arrived home in great distress, saying that he would never try counselling again. She said that he had felt misunderstood – as usual – but, worse, he had felt mocked, and by someone who professed to offer help. I realised that I had totally failed to enter Devendra's frame of reference, had failed to understand his unusual way of processing, had assumed he was talking in my language and was not trying to convey anything of 'real importance' in that initial session. In fact, he was desperately hoping that a supposed 'helper' could understand what agonies he was experiencing in his isolation. I didn't recognise that, for him, any opportunity to relate was a risk, but he was prepared to take that risk. Rather than assuming that we would communicate using my language I should have encountered him in his reality – discovering his language. My apprehension about meeting a new – rather unusual – client meant that I became stuck in my own frame of reference.

To protect the client, and ourselves, we must stay in touch with our own realities, be aware of our boundaries and limits and be clear with the client about them – and must not continue with work we find too difficult. Our quality of presence will deteriorate if we start merely to portray, rather than 'be', the therapist conditions. If a client fighting to retain a sense of self becomes aware of any incongruence on our part, it will only add to feelings of fragmentation, alienation, barrenness and panic and confirm that relationships are untrustworthy and unreliable.

When it Goes Right

Behaviours that seem peculiar to others may be the individual's attempt to impose some sense of control on their sense of self and their experience. People can appear to create another world to live in, or to withdraw from the world or relationships – even those relationships that 'should' be the closest and that 'should' offer unconditional love and support. If relationships are discussed as the client experiences them, the person's withdrawal often makes sense as a way of protecting themselves, as illustrated in the next vignette.

Kayleigh

Kayleigh wanted to talk about how her sister (for whom she felt responsible) had been sexually abused as a child by their father and his friends. For some fifteen minutes of the session, I could not shake the feeling that she was, in fact, talking about herself, as she had spoken before of being an only child. This questioning was filling my head until I realised that it didn't matter whether the sister existed or not. I felt a physical change within me and I was suddenly able to remain empathically within Kayleigh's frame of reference, so understanding her idiosyncratic meaning. That feeling of – finally – being heard helped her to address much of the pain, confusion and disgust she felt around her own abuse. Once we got to that point she was able to talk about it and began to develop a new sense of self that integrated her past and had more meaning for her as the woman she was becoming.

Dissociating – seeing oneself as separate – from previous or current experiences is often used as a defence against some dreadful experience. When one realises that Kayleigh has created a 'sister' to dissociate herself from the trauma of the sexual abuse, we see that it makes perfect sense to use that form of protection. Separating herself from it is how she coped with it at the time.

By accepting the reality of the dissociated experience the therapist enables clients to explore the meaning of it at a safe distance. Clients can be empathic to themselves by retaining the 'as if' quality when exploring their own experiences. That distance, in the presence of a non-judgemental, genuine listener who also seems to understand the experience, creates a safe environment for clients finally to look at, and then integrate, childhood trauma or abuse into realistic, adult selves.

On Becoming a Patient

Withdrawal from a shared reality, isolation and diminished social functioning can be the results of an inability to express one's experiencing in a way that makes sense to others or to the cultural values one holds oneself. Sometimes people are aware that others do not understand them or share their realities and, perhaps, they do not understand themselves. For some, this can lead to the imposition of a medical diagnosis and consequent 'treatment' to restore the individual to some assumed level of 'normality'. This can include enforced hospitalisation as in the examples below.

Joan and Ruby

In one of the daily community meetings on the acute psychiatric ward Joan said that she was going out with the lifeboat crew that day. She'd already whispered to everyone that the occupational therapist was with the CIA and that her mother had had her identity card shredded by the Navy because they didn't like what she knew. The main response was laughter or a glossing over it, but certainly no engagement. Staff told me later that she is what is termed a 'revolving door patient' and was currently 'very unwell'. She would remain on the ward until her medication started to work and she became 'more settled', then she would be discharged and would stay out until she stopped taking her medication, which would inevitably mean that she stopped taking care of herself. Then she would be brought in again. I was told that it was best not to engage with her comments as it 'only fuelled the delusions'. I was told the same about Ruby, who said that her son, Will Smith, would be visiting that Sunday as it was Mother's Day.

The fact that Joan and Ruby could not cope outside the hospital for any length of time implies that they find something in life a struggle. But they have not been offered the opportunity to work on accepting their ways of being, or to deal differently with difficulties. That is not meant (entirely) as a criticism of mainstream psychiatric care. Nursing staff are too busy to talk at length with people individually and counselling provision is very limited.

From Patient to Person

In placing the 'person' at the centre of the therapeutic process the person-centred approach avoids objectifying the client as a 'patient'. Consider the following accounts drawn from the stories of a number of people, including Janice Hartley (Hartley, 2008).

Patient 1

Patient 1 was diagnosed as schizophrenic after a psychotic breakdown. His father had also suffered from delusions and disordered thought. After his wife was involved in a road accident he had become unwell, eventually staying out all night in a forest. On his return home the following day he reported that he had been talking to the animals and plants that had kept him safe when he couldn't find his way home. He was admitted to a psychiatric hospital but was not compliant with the staff about taking his prescribed medication, and was disruptive on the ward and would not accept that he was ill. He absconded and was found walking along the streets in his nightclothes near his home. He was therefore considered to be at risk of harming himself and to be incapable of caring properly for himself, and so he was detained under the Mental Health Act. After eight weeks of taking his medication in hospital he became more settled and was discharged home.

Person 1

Person 1 had always coped with a busy life, helping others, since his mother had demanded he take on the role of man of the house at the age of ten when his father died. When his wife was seriously injured in a road accident he suddenly had the extra responsibility of caring for her as well as their four children and his mother, maintaining a full-time job and continuing to coach his son's football team. After a while he started to become resentful and very tired. One day he wanted a break and so he went for a walk in the forest. But he kept walking till it was dark and couldn't find his way back. He was so deep in the forest that his mobile phone didn't work so that he couldn't ring home either. But he felt fine and suddenly realised that he could communicate with all the plants, trees and animals. He felt at peace for the first time: he belonged there.

In the morning he arrived home to discover his mother and the police there. They were all angry with him. He couldn't understand it; he was fine. The break had helped him to feel calm and had restored his energy to cope with the struggles in his life. But everyone insisted that he go to hospital. He agreed because he was quite tired and felt that he could do with another couple of days of rest. And it seemed to make people more distressed if he objected anyway. Once in the hospital he felt odd, so he thought he should check that he had been given the right medication. He thought that he would be safer near the floor in case he passed out and so crawled to the nurses' station. For some reason this upset the staff and he was angrily told to get back into bed and to stay there. But he knew that he couldn't stay there as his family needed him at home. They had taken his shoes away so he took someone else's, put on his dressing gown so that he didn't get cold, and set off so that he could walk home before the children got back from school. After being picked up by the police two miles from his home, he was forced to stay in the hospital for the next eight weeks until staff accepted that the medication had eradicated his delusions.

Clearly, Patient 1 and Person 1 are the same man – Graham. But his 'odd' behaviour makes sense when considered in the light of the second account.

Graham

Graham began person-centred therapy on being discharged from hospital and also managed to access help with care for his wife and children. He believes that his person-centred therapist has accompanied him along a path of exploration and he feels her respectful, non-judgemental attitude has helped him to integrate and embrace his experiences as a spiritual awakening rather than as an episode of madness. He has worked out who he is, and how he wants to live. He is more able to take his place in his relationships now rather than always trying to be what others want him to be.

As professionals we are also the product of our upbringing and society. A self-structure (including our notions about the world) under threat becomes more rigid (Proposition XVI). So a self-structure that is based on traditional ideas of mental illness is unlikely readily to accept that a 'patient' displaying a difficult or unusual way of being could be the expert in his own process during his time of crisis. No one asked Graham what meanings events had for him, and the medical authorities' extra justification for acting as experts in this case was that Graham's father had been diagnosed with schizophrenia some twenty-five years previously.

Conclusion: Finding the Method in the Madness

Sometimes therapy involves a re-evaluation of elements of the self-concept, sometimes not. Some people feel supported by medication, some may welcome sojourns in hospital if they feel themselves starting to disintegrate or to fragment. What matters is that people retain responsibility for their own processes, for their own recoveries and for their own lives. It seems that, in many contexts, the person-centred values of unconditional positive regard, empathy and congruence appear to offer help and healing. The argument about medical versus non-medical ways of understanding different realities is irrelevant because people attach unique meanings to their experiences – illness, disease, reactions to life events or spiritual journeys, to name but a few. But the socially stigmatising attitudes that accompany descriptions of unusual ways of being as mental illness are very damaging to people already feeling vulnerable and under stress. The vignette below shows that just to be 'held' in a fragile state can be healing and can be the start of the journey back to re-integration.

Rifat

For a period of time during her twenties Rifat says that there was no 'her' and that she had lost the ability to relate to herself or to others. She wasn't distressed and saw no need for therapy, but talks of 'odd thinking patterns and behaviours'. She calls it her 'psychotic episode' and says that she describes it as an illness because she was unwell. Even after forty years she remembers a person who took care of her and accepted her without judgement. This person seemed to understand her and had a profound effect on helping her start to re-establish a connection with the world in a way that suited her pace and her needs. It was not in the context of a formal therapeutic relationship but the values were certainly person-centred.

Not all clients can, or wish to, undertake self-exploration leading to personal development that facilitates self-reliance in the modern world. Some people find healing in the experience of a genuine, empathic relationship where they are accepted as they are. Similarly, it can be therapeutic just to be offered unconditional, concrete, practical assistance. This goes to the heart of the person-centred approach in trusting the client as expert and not having an agenda for change. So often psychiatric treatment aims to 'cure' clients so that they conform to some externally defined normality or way of functioning.

If we accept that everyone has their own neurological/psychological makeup, and, work in a truly person-centred way with individual realities, I suggest that each individual will actualise as best they can – will find the method in their 'madness'.

Notes

1 All vignettes are fictional composites of two or more people.
2 My thanks go to Dr Clive Perrett for his time and insights that have helped my understanding enormously.

Guide to Further Reading

Freeth, R. (2007) *Humanising Psychiatry and Mental Health Care: The Challenge of the Person-Centred Approach*. Oxford: Radcliffe Publishing.

Joseph, S. and Worsley, R. (eds) (2005) *Person-Centred Psychopathology: A Positive Psychology of Mental Health*. Ross-on-Wye: PCCS Books.

Lambers, E. (2003) 'Person-centred psychopathology', in D. Mearns, *Developing Person-Centred Counselling*. London: Sage, pp. 103–19.

Warner, M.S. (2000) 'Person-centred therapy at the difficult edge: A developmentally based model of fragile and dissociated process', in D. Mearns and B. Thorne (eds), *Person-Centred Therapy Today: New Frontiers in Theory and Practice*. London: Sage, pp. 144–71.

These works contain useful discussions and explanations of different types of processes linking person-centred thinking to mainstream psychiatric and biomedical positions.

Sanders, P. and Tudor, K. (2001) 'This is therapy: A person-centred critique of the contemporary psychiatric system', in C. Newnes, G. Holmes and C. Dunn (eds), *This is Madness too: Critical Perspectives on Mental Health Services*. Ross-on-Wye: PCCS Books, pp. 147–60.

Sommerbeck, L. (2003) *The Client-Centred Therapist in Psychiatric Contexts: A Therapists' Guide to the Psychiatric Landscape and its Inhabitants.* Ross-on-Wye: PCCS Books.

These two works demonstrate person-centred ways of understanding and working within psychiatric contexts, highlighting tensions and possibilities for person-centred practitioners.

Sanders, P. (2007) 'Schizophrenia is not an illness: A response to van Blarikom,' *Person-Centered & Experiential Psychotherapies*, 6 (2): 112–28.

Van Blarikom, J. (2006) 'A person-centered approach to schizophrenia,' *Person-Centered & Experiential Therapies*, 5 (3): 155–73.

An interesting debate between different person-centred approaches to one type of 'mental illness'.

References

Hartley, J. (2008) 'Mapping the far side of the mind: Psychosis and recovery as an inner spiritual journey', paper presented at Asylum! Conference and Festival, Manchester Metropolitan University, 10–12 September.

Mearns, D. and Cooper, M. (2005) *Working at Relational Depth in Counselling and Psychotherapy*. London: Sage.

Prouty, G., Pörtner, M. and Van Werde, D. (2002) *Pre-Therapy: Reaching Contact-Impaired Clients*. Ross-on-Wye: PCCS Books.

Rogers, C.R. (1951) 'A theory of personality and behaviour', in C.R. Rogers, *Client-Centered Therapy*. Boston, MA: Houghton Mifflin, pp. 481–533.

Rogers, C.R. (1959) 'A theory of therapy, personality and interpersonal relationships as developed in the client-centered framework', in S. Koch (ed.), *Psychology: A Study of Science*, Vol. 3. *Formulations of the Person and the Social Context*. New York: McGraw-Hill: pp. 184–256.

Rogers, C.R. (1961) 'A process conception of psychotherapy', in C.R. Rogers, *On Becoming a Person: A Therapist's View of Psychotherapy*. London: Constable, pp. 125–59.

Warner, M.S. (2006) 'Towards an integrated person-centered theory of wellness and psychopathology', *Person-Centered & Experiential Psychotherapies*, 5 (1): 4–20.

Warner, M.S. (2007) 'Luke's process: A positive view of schizophrenic thought disorder', in R. Worsley and S. Joseph (eds), *Person-Centred Practice: Case Studies in Positive Psychology*. Ross-on-Wye: PCCS Books, pp. 142–55.

PART THREE

Behavioural Reactions to Life Events

8

WORKING WITH DRUG AND ALCOHOL ISSUES

ROSE CAMERON

A Person-Centred Understanding of Excessive Drug or Alcohol Use

Working with a client who seems hell-bent on letting their use of alcohol or another drug wreck their health, their employability and their relationships and even deprive them of the most basic necessities, not to mention their dignity, can be dispiriting and confusing without a clear theoretical understanding of the processes leading to and away from such excessive substance use. Unlike most other humanistic and psychodynamic schools of therapy, person-centred therapy (PCT) admits no drive towards atrophy or destruction, but anyone who has watched someone consistently use a substance to a degree that distresses and angers their loved ones, renders them unemployable, causes them to risk imprisonment, may eventually destroy every organ in their body or result in permanent brain damage *and* be abjectly miserable in the process, may be forgiven for concluding that the actualising tendency cannot be at work in someone this self-destructive. This chapter sets out to demonstrate that indeed it is, and explores some of the issues that may arise in working with excessive alcohol or drug use from a person-centred perspective.

Rogers (Proposition XII, 1951; 507) discusses how some needs are denied symbolisation in awareness if incompatible with the self-concept. The next Proposition (XIII, Rogers 1951: 509) implies that sometimes we find ourselves doing something that we think that we should not, or cannot, and then saying, and believing, that 'it wasn't me', or 'something took me over'.

The 'something' was the actualising tendency pressing to meet an organismic need. Alcohol and other mood-altering drugs facilitate this process.

Alcohol softens the control exercised by the self-structure. We become chattier, or more outrageous, or aggressive, or more prone to tears, doing things under the influence that we would not normally do. People who use substances problematically often do so because what they are using frees denied feelings or denied aspects of themselves. This can be seen in the following example.

Brenda

Brenda had a lengthy criminal record. All her offences had been committed while she was drunk. She talked with amazement about how she 'just took things' when drunk, and saw herself as 'a different person' when doing so. Her manner, when sober, was particularly self-effacing and diffident and, as we worked together, it became evident that she had very little awareness of having any needs or desires. Drinking allowed Brenda to take what she wanted, without having to acknowledge her needs or change her self-concept.

Disinhibition is particularly characteristic of alcohol but not necessarily of other mood-altering drugs, yet these too may meet a denied need. Heroin, for example, is a very powerful painkiller, as effective an anaesthetic for emotional pain as for physical pain. Not only do substances help the user to meet denied needs, but they also help to ease the psychological tension that arises from denying them. The greater the incongruence between the self-structure and organismic experience, the greater the internal pressure to satisfy denied needs, creating ever more psychological tension. Drugs like heroin that depress the central nervous system (CNS) promote a feeling of relaxation. The discomfort of the psychological tension that results from incongruence is eased as the client begins to feel warm, sleepy and relaxed. Stimulants like amphetamines also ease psychological tension. Margaret Warner, writing about 'low intensity fragile process' (see Mearns and Thorne 2000: 147) suggests that un-integrated aspects of the self may result in a lack of energy and a feeling of emptiness, rather than anxiety. Psychological tension characterised by depression can be eased by stimulants that make the user feel full of life. However, using a substance in order to reduce or to tolerate incongruence only helps in the short term. In the longer term, the individual will not experience satisfaction of the underlying need until it is acknowledged and integrated into the self-structure. Continued denial of organismic needs is easier if the need-seeking behaviour can be attributed to the effect of a mind-altering substance ('it was the drink talking'). In this way the incongruence is ultimately prolonged and intensified.

Excessive substance use eases psychological tension in some ways but can also increase it. The person who uses alcohol to help meet a denied need or liberate a denied aspect of themselves may well feel ashamed afterwards, leading to an increase in psychological tension. The cultural context in which the drug is used may give rise to feelings of shame and worthlessness. Crack, for instance, has a particularly low social status and users often feel especially ashamed that they use it. Some people feel ashamed that they are using an illegal drug at all, and drug users and drinkers often do things that they are ashamed of to obtain their substance. In addition to feelings of shame, the chemical after-effects of many substances leave the person depressed and anxious. Shame, fear of being caught and 'coming down' all create more psychological tension and an increased desire for the feelings of relief produced by taking something. A self-perpetuating cycle may ensue, in which the person 'uses' to ease psychological tension, feels wonderful (or at least better) whilst under the influence, but even more anxious when the effect wears off, and is more inclined to seek relief through being under the influence.

Although most drugs create a psychological – rather than a physical – dependence, some, like heroin and alcohol, are also physically addictive, creating a self-perpetuating need for relief from the unpleasant, and sometimes dangerous, physical symptoms of withdrawal. Using a mood-altering substance to ease psychological tension is an initially effective solution for many people but one that is likely to create a lot more problems than it ever solved. It is precisely this that, paradoxically, makes it hard not to use more. The immediate relief from pain is a more attractive prospect than the long and difficult process of resuming self-responsibility. Facing the demons that preceded the problematic drinking or using, and which multiply during it is, a daunting prospect.

The process of change

Constructive change begins when the client perceives the counsellor (or other practitioner) to be genuinely empathic and unconditionally accepting. This enables clients to become more accepting of organismic experience previously masked by substance use. However, there is an ever-present danger that, as the client becomes more aware of underlying psychological tension, the internal pressure to use again, or use more, will become overwhelming. When this happens, the discomfort of the original incongruence is eased and so the client's internal motivation to work with it therapeutically decreases and the motivation to deal with incongruence by using drugs or drink increases. The client who stops or reduces drug or alcohol use and takes time to adjust to this before exploring very sensitive issues, gives him- or herself the best chance of working through these without resuming their previous habit. Person-centred theory suggests that a counsellor's aim in working with drug and alcohol issues is to reduce the psychological tension that created the need for substance use in the first place. Practice, however, suggests that underlying issues may often only be reached by edging very carefully along a precipice.

A client may come into therapy with no awareness that their substance use is causing problems, or they may be aware and:

- Want to change their use.
- Not want to change it.
- Want to change it but find themselves unable to.

Obviously the needs of a client at these stages will be different. Although the ultimate aim of a person-centred therapist in addressing drug and alcohol issues is to resolve pre-existing psychological tensions, the client may be a long way from being ready to work at such an unsettling level. Understanding and respecting the client's process of coming to terms with a substance problem is an essential foundation to offering a relationship that is neither pushy nor collusive.

Denial

It is likely that at some point the fact that the client feels they *need* the substance and finds it difficult to function without it, becomes shameful in itself. The client's focus moves from denying the primary needs resulting in underlying incongruence to denying the need-satisfying behaviour. The substance user may enter a period of denial, hiding evidence of their use even if living alone. Although it would be a contradiction for someone in denial of a substance problem to seek help with it, it is not uncommon for a client who is denying such a problem to seek help with something else. This point is exemplified below.

Chris

In her initial session, Chris voiced a number of issues. Most aspects of life were proving difficult in some way and although I listened carefully to the specific aspects of each difficulty, I was burningly aware that each ended with a coda of 'because I was drunk', or 'because I was hungover'. I did not want to impose my own perception but I had a hunch that Chris would perceive directness as respectful and anything less as patronising. When I said, 'It sounds like you're saying drink is playing a major role in all these problems,' she looked genuinely astonished. She sat in deep thought for a few moments, then said, 'I am, aren't I? Well, I'll stop.' And she did.

Bill

I had been seeing Bill for some time and was increasingly unsure as to why he was coming. He had stopped talking about his presenting problem and his sessions were becoming monologues about his week. I gathered from the concerns of his GP that drinking was an issue and wondered, when he came to a session smelling strongly of drink, if he was trying to drop a hint that he wanted me to pick up. I voiced my thoughts; he was outraged and our relationship never fully recovered.

Although both were in denial about their drinking, Chris was, in terms of Rogers' seven stages of process, at Stage 4 whilst Bill was at Stage 1. Chris had a high degree of self-acceptance and was ready and able to perceive herself more accurately. Bill was still using alcohol to pacify the first inklings of the anxiety and awareness of tension that would move him to Stage 2. He was simply not ready to acknowledge his drinking as a problem.

Awareness

Some clients are aware that their use of a substance is a problem but do not want, or do not feel able, to reduce or stop it. They sometimes choose to remain in therapy. Some will talk about their use and some will not. The inexperienced counsellor may be tempted to push the client subtly towards change. However, there is little point in this. In person-centred terms, the client will recognise the need to change only when prompted to do so by their organismic experience. Pressure from the counsellor, however subtle or well intentioned, risks damaging the therapeutic relationship.

A client who feels that their substance use is spiralling out of control is likely to feel alarmed and may just want to focus on stopping or reducing use. Some will want to know *how* they should do this. Although it is contrary to the therapeutic aims of the PCA to direct a client's process, this is not the case with other approaches. If the client really feels the need for a structure at this stage, the most respectful thing to do might be to refer them to an agency that offers one. Holding onto an externally created structure like Alcoholics Anonymous's Twelve-Step Programme can be literally life-saving for someone who feels that they are no longer able to control their compulsion to drink or shoot up.

Withdrawal

Some clients do feel able to work out their own way of stopping or reducing drug use within a person-centred relationship and so feel no need for an external structure. If the counsellor is the main or sole source of support for such a client, it is particularly important that both are aware that it can be dangerous suddenly to stop using certain substances (namely alcohol, barbiturates and benzodiazepines), and that they know when and how to access medical support. The local drug and alcohol team, hospital or the client's GP should be able to advise on this. Most clients will not be risking their lives if they stop drinking or using drugs without medical care but those who do not think they will manage to stop on their own, or who are fearful of experiencing the withdrawal symptoms whilst alone, may prefer inpatient care. Others may prefer to stay at home and take medication (known as a 'home detox'). Some alcohol and drug agencies, as well as GPs, offer support and guidance during a home detox. Whatever a client is detoxifying from and whether they are taking medication or not, it is a good idea if someone keeps an eye on them. Being by the client's side continually whilst they withdraw is obviously beyond the usual boundaries of the counselling relationship but long-standing members of a Twelve Step group may well be willing to do this.

Not all drugs are physically addictive. Drugs that create physical dependence, leading to unpleasant or dangerous physical symptoms when the body is deprived of them, are drugs such as opiates which depress the central nervous system (CNS); and drugs that have a pain-killing effect. Drugs that stimulate the CNS system are not physically addictive. Stimulants differ from depressants and painkillers in that they cannot be used continually over a very long period – they produce unpleasant effects if used in excess, and euphoria is replaced by paranoia, aliveness by anxiety. The unpleasant effects of excessive stimulant-use are a result of the organism having had too much rather than having to do without but they may nevertheless last for quite some time. Someone who has used too much stimulant may feel very agitated for weeks.

This does not necessarily mean that stimulants are less compulsive than physically addictive drugs. Crack is not physically addictive but it is probably the most compulsive drug because of the intensity of both the high and the comedown. The comedown is so unpleasant that many people use heroin to lessen its severity. Hallucinogens are neither physically nor psychologically addictive. Issues relating to their use are more likely to concern experiences that the client had under their influence than dependence on them.

Maintaining change – the early stages

The psychological and emotional aspects of doing without alcohol or other drugs can be just as unpleasant and difficult as the physical effects (perhaps more so) and they last much longer. The psychological tension that made the substance attractive in the first place remains after its effects have worn off. Additionally, the person who has been using heavily or for a long time is almost certainly less well-equipped to face a difficult emotional process than they were before they started using. People who consider that they have a problem with a substance almost always feel a great deal of shame. They may also feel deeply ashamed of their behaviour when under the influence, seeking the influence or recovering from it. Their self-esteem is likely to be very low and it may be that they have lost much, or even all, of their support system of family and friends. It may be difficult for a client to work on emotionally stirring issues without wanting to drink or use their drug at this stage and so it is important to be in constant collaboration as to how deeply to work. Some clients may not be ready to look at difficult issues for quite a long time.

For the first few months of being without it, most people who have been relying heavily on a substance struggle just to get through the day. At this stage a client may well need the containment of an external structure because the deeper wisdom of their actualising tendency is constantly at risk of being drowned out by shrieks of withdrawal, craving, shame and pre-existing pain – and the knowledge that drinking or using again would just stop it all. Somebody who has been heavily reliant may simply not have access to the inner resources to enable them to take care of themselves twenty-four hours a day and will need more support than the counsellor can give. There is a lot of support available. Clients who want very intensive support might benefit from a residential facility and many choose to go to away from their own area so that they are not near their old haunts and drinking/using companions. Clients who do not want such intensive support but need more than the counsellor can offer may find Twelve Step meetings or support groups run by local agencies helpful. Most areas have multidisciplinary alcohol and drug teams that can be consulted about local and national resources.

Maintaining change – the later stages

Therapy can be particularly helpful at this stage because it enables the client to look at the underlying reasons for their excessive use in a way that other models of helping people who use problematically do not. However, a client who has stopped heavy use of a substance is likely to feel very fragile for some months after and caution should be exercised in working on sensitive issues. It may be a long while before clients are ready to look at some of the root causes behind their need to use. Clients who are in this position for the first time may not appreciate how easily overwhelmed they may become and so it may be well worth inviting them to double-check with themselves that they feel ready before working with anything potentially stirring.

Drinking or using drugs again

It is an interesting reflection of our cultural attitudes that the idea of a heroin or crack addict giving up with the hope of being able to use again at some point in the future seems bizarre, whilst the idea of someone who has had an alcohol problem never being able to drink again seems extreme. Can someone who has had a problem with alcohol drink again without the problem recurring? I believe that whether a particular client can return to social drinking is something that can only be decided by experience and I doubt that, for many, the experiment would be worthwhile. This belief is based on experience and observation rather than theory. Whilst person-centred theory implies that someone who has resolved the underlying psychological tension leading to excessive use could drink moderately in the future, my experience suggests that this is not always the case. I have worked with problem drinkers at every stage of intoxication and sobriety and my overwhelming impression has been that alcohol, even in small quantities, affects some people in an extreme way and that drinking in moderation is not possible for everyone.

Generally, the question of returning to recreational use is not as common with drug use because the social pressure to use drugs is not as culturally pervasive as the pressure to drink. However, a client may want to resume having the occasional 'E' or line of cocaine or smoking the odd joint. If the client has not resolved the issues that led to them using excessively, the likelihood of their use spiralling out of control again is high. If the client considers that they *have* managed to resolve the issues underlying their excessive use, they may choose to risk recreational use but, of course, there are no guarantees that they will be able to use moderately. A client may drink or use drugs again not because they believe that they can do so without their use spiralling out of control but because their craving is already out of control and they have acted on it rather than their overall intent to abstain. Their use may be a brief episode after which they stop again or they may continue to use and stay in counselling.

The Six Conditions in Practice

Perhaps the most controversial dilemma in the practice of working with someone who is concerned about their substance use is whether or not to see them when they are under the influence. Some practitioners are prevented from doing this by their employing agency. Others feel that they would not be able to make sufficient psychological contact with such a client and make a prior agreement that in such circumstances the appointment will be cancelled. It is certainly true that the *quality* of psychological contact will be affected if the client is under the influence of a mood-altering substance. However, psychological contact involves each person being affected *in some way* by the other's presence, so being under the influence will not prevent *some* psychological contact – unless the client is actually unconscious. It seems fair to assume that a client who is incoherent and unable to see straight (although in some way impacted by the counsellor's presence) will not be able to use the session in the usual way, but the counsellor's continued acceptance of them, even when under the influence and presenting in a way that they find shameful, may be therapeutic.

The question of psychological contact concerns not only clients whose state is highly altered but also clients who are more moderately affected by what they have taken. Some clients may need some alcohol or something else just to feel well enough to get to the session – it may be the case that sufficient psychological contact only becomes possible if the client *has* used something. There is a continuum between the client being too psychologically altered and altered just enough, along which the quality of psychological contact will vary.

Person-centred theory suggests no absolute prohibition on seeing a client who is under the influence. Each counsellor, unless constrained by the rules of an agency, has the freedom and responsibility to set their own boundaries to protect themselves and their clients. I now work from home and discuss with a potential client who is drinking very regularly and heavily whether they are likely to turn up drunk on my doorstep outside session times before I agree to work with them. It may seem naive of me to trust the word of a sober person regarding what they will not do when drunk. Whenever I have asked, the client has assured me that they will not turn up unexpectedly and their non-verbal communication has been utterly congruent with the verbal. I believe that I have sufficient experience of working with people who use or have used excessively to sense if someone were not able to respect my boundaries, but it remains a risk.

Rose

I once worked on a project for crude-spirit drinkers and inadvertently moved into a flat on the route between the project and one of the shops where clients bought their drink. My concerns about the clients, who were very demanding of my attention when I was at work, realising where I lived and banging on my door when drunk (or sober), evaporated when I realised that they were pretending that they hadn't seen me if we happened to be in the street at the same time. In general they showed great respect for my privacy and only one client ever rolled up drunk on my doorstep. I didn't answer the door, and it never happened again.

There are two levels of client incongruence that are important in working with someone with a substance problem – the underlying incongruence that motivated the excessive use and the incongruence that results from repeatedly doing something that becomes increasingly harmful. A client who is successfully using alcohol or drugs to mask underlying incongruence will, by definition, be unaware of this incongruence or the inner tension it is causing. They will not be motivated to work on it, which if they are still using or drinking, may be just as well since they are likely to be too emotionally fragile to work with difficult issues without increasing their use. They may experience the incongruence and discomfort that will move them from the first to the second stage of process only when drinking or using stops working and begins to create more problems than it solves. If drinking or using a drug is still solving more problems than it is creating, the client will be unlikely to want to change.

Clients who have stopped drinking or using are likely to become acutely aware of the anxiety caused by underlying incongruence as they are no longer quietening it down chemically. They may not know much about the nature of the incongruence but will know something is not right. In allowing themselves to be aware of this they will take a beginning step in the process of change.

Geoff

Geoff had stopped drinking because he realised that he had begun to experience withdrawal symptoms in the mornings – sweating, trembling and anxiety. His GP referred him for counselling four months after he had stopped because he was still experiencing acute anxiety. Geoff knew that anxiety is one of the withdrawal symptoms from alcohol and had expected to feel anxious during the physical detoxification period but couldn't understand why he was still anxious four months on. He began to discover the answer when he explored a faint awareness of feeling stressed at work. When he and his counsellor explored this further he realised that he had begun drinking heavily after work not just because that was a part of his workplace culture but also because he had been more stressed than he realised. After several sessions he realised that he was actually frightened of the enthusiastic and motivating manager he so admired. Geoff was eventually able to accept that he couldn't meet the continually moving targets that his manager set, and the work he did around his fear of letting someone down yielded changes in his personal as well as his work life.

As a result of hiding their use, most heavy alcohol or drug users become expert in the art of deceit and can detect incongruence with paranormal speed and accuracy. They are also likely to be particularly sensitive to judgement and be highly sensitised to the counsellor's every reaction. It may be tempting to try to hide a reaction of disgust or disappointment so as not to shame the client further but it is probable that the client's skill in detecting incongruence will outweigh the counsellor's skill in hiding it. Genuineness has mattered more than any other quality to all the drinkers and drug users that I have ever worked with.

Mark

Mark, a client in the re-hab centre where I worked, had engaged my and the residents' protective feelings by talking haltingly in group meetings about how he didn't feel good enough to be with 'you nice people' after living on the streets. Everybody liked this vulnerable but brave man and we all felt very uncomfortable and awkward when it became evident that he hadn't changed his clothes for over a week and had begun to smell. Mark had talked about the abuse he had endured on the streets and how casual remarks about him being a smelly old tramp had been as painful to him as the physical abuse. I was terrified of hurting or humiliating him but when he began an individual session with me by saying that he had sensed a subtle difference in how I was with him, I knew that it was because I was trying not to breathe in the smell and that not breathing easily was making me tense. I said that I still felt huge warmth towards him and really liked him but I was aware that I was beginning not to like the smell of his clothes, which made me want to keep away from him, and that I had been frightened to say so in case I hurt his feelings. Mark had a mixture of feelings in response. He was embarrassed. He was also surprised as he never changed his clothes more than once a week in his life. So we talked about how central heating, which he'd never experienced before, can make you sweat even in winter and how general standards of hygiene had changed since he was young. His strongest feelings were of relief that he hadn't offended me or 'done anything wrong', and when he thanked me for being honest with him the relief we both felt drew us closer together.

The counsellor's awareness of their flow of experience and a willingness to be open about it is also important because problematic substance use is as much a style of relating as a way of dealing with inner tension. Some heavy users control and manipulate those around them by, for instance, becoming aggressive so that they have an excuse to drink or use, behaving in a frightening or pitiful way when under the influence or abdicating responsibility for themselves. Heavy users are often controlled and manipulated by those around them, perhaps by being obliged to make themselves sexually available to a dealer or by being encouraged to become dependent so that they are more malleable. Not all controlling or manipulative behaviour is maliciously intended. Many partners try to control their spouse's consumption or attempt to limit or repair the damage that they do. This is ultimately unhelpful because it prevents the person from experiencing the consequences of what they are doing and discourages them from taking responsibility for themselves. They are interrupting a process that might lead to sufficient discomfort to provoke change. Whether punitive or sympathetic in tone, external control is disempowering.

The relationships formed between someone who is using heavily and those around them are complex, and, at some level, suit both parties. Many friends, relatives and colleagues have more of a problem with the drinker or user after they stop using and start trying to resume responsibility for themselves than they had before. Clients trying to stop or reduce problematic substance use or stay stopped will probably have to change the way that they relate to other people if they are to be successful. Personal power cannot be taken without consent and although the client may resent attempts to control their behaviour they may at the same time be inviting the other person to be controlling. It is to be hoped that a client who is behaving in this way towards other people in their lives will also behave in this way in therapy. Bringing typical behaviour and ways of relating directly into the therapeutic frame in this way provides an opportunity to examine them in the safety of the therapeutic relationship. The counsellor can help the client become more aware of how they relate to other people by sharing their reactions. It is important that the counsellor is sensitively attuned to their process in order to be aware of *feeling* manipulated rather than actually *being* manipulated. Many users may already have had a lot of feedback about how they relate to others from those around them but often it will have been harsh and judgemental because the person giving it was angry or hurt. The counsellor is in a unique position of intimacy without involvement in the client's life and well equipped to give feedback that is helpful rather than just hurtful.

Paula

Paula was very anxious and although she had stopped using three years previously her family still showed little respect for her or patience with her timidity. She was tearfully recounting an incident in which her son had called her 'pathetic', and somewhat dramatically started wailing about how right he was, what a terrible mother she was, what a worthless human being, the worst person in the world. After some minutes of this she looked at her counsellor a little expectantly and, almost helping her along, said with a sigh that she knew that she shouldn't 'beat herself up'. Her counsellor, Suzanne, surprised her by saying that she wondered if Paula really was 'beating herself up'. Suzanne said she'd felt quite detached whilst Paula was proclaiming her worthlessness, as if she was watching someone do something for effect rather than because they genuinely felt it in the moment. Paula was not pleased by Suzanne's response, but it did bring a more immediate and authentic quality to their relationship and in time Paula was able to recognise how manipulated her family felt by her frequent displays of helplessness.

For the counsellor, difficulty in staying alongside the client usually arises from the counsellor's own agenda or investment. Investments differ from agendas in that they are more emotionally charged. Not only does the counsellor think that the client should follow a particular course of action but also there is an emotional pay-off for the counsellor if the client does so. Investments are usually much more subtle than agendas, and the counsellor less aware of them. They are very likely to be present if the counsellor has, or has had, a close relationship in their own life with someone using heavily. Those who have had such relationships often imagine that their experience and knowledge place them at an advantage in working with a client who has an alcohol or drug problem. Unfortunately, any advantage will almost certainly be outweighed by the fact that they will have developed ways of relating to the person in their own life that are likely to re-emerge and adversely affect the counselling relationship. If, for instance, the counsellor was brought up by, or has lived with, someone with a substance abuse problem, it is likely that they will have developed a tendency to take responsibility for others, especially if their lives seem chaotic. The counsellor must recognise and work through the effect that someone else's substance abuse has had on them, and work through their feelings towards that person if they are to avoid getting in the way of their client's process.

A similar principle applies to counsellors who have had a problem with alcohol or drugs themselves. It is true that anyone who has experienced dependence on a substance is well equipped to empathise, but equally true that they are at risk of identifying rather than empathising. It is also very likely that they will want the client to stop successfully, like they did, and that they will have a strong investment in whatever process worked for them.

Maintaining unconditional positive regard can be challenging when working with a client who is behaving in a way that seems very self-destructive. Other people in the client's life may use judgement, dismissal and psychological withdrawal as a means of lessening the pain of watching their loved one self-destruct but the person-centred counsellor is committed to contact with and acceptance of the person however they behave. This can be challenging, not just because it is painful to stay emotionally connected to people who are hurting themselves but also because full and unconditional acceptance of the client however they behave means not minimising their behaviour. There may be a temptation, particularly for an inexperienced counsellor, to minimise their client's behaviour in order to ameliorate their shame. However, unconditional acceptance involves seeing and accepting the reality of the behaviour and still maintaining positive regard for the person, whatever they do. If the counsellor minimises the client's behaviour in order to reduce the client's shame, the client will be impeded in their therapeutic need to symbolise their experience without distortion and accept themselves more fully. Shame and guilt are not always inappropriate or damaging. Acknowledging the hurt that they have caused and feeling ashamed, guilty or sad may be the first step in the client's process of remorse, amends, forgiveness and resolution. If the feelings of shame are not fully accepted this process becomes stuck and the client is not able to move on. It is important, if we catch ourselves wanting to mini-mise, that we explore where such a need may come from in ourselves.

Niki

My supervisee, Niki, was telling me about Julie, who had broken her baby's arm whilst drunk. She became very distressed at the thought of the baby being in pain and unable to get help. I asked whether she'd felt this distressed in the session and she said that she had just felt sorry for Julie and told her that she was sure that she had only done it because she was drunk and had agreed with her that Social Services were being unjust in continuing to keep the baby in care. I had not heard anything to suggest that Julie had any appreciation at all of the enormity of what she had done and asked Niki why she was so sure that Julie would parent safely enough when sober. Niki realised that she wasn't sure of this at all. When we explored the pity that she had felt for Julie, it transpired that Niki was so shocked that she'd over-compensated so that Julie would not feel judged. I suggested that Niki look at this in her own therapy and she slowly uncovered a long-standing pattern of hiding anger and disapproval in case she offended anyone who may then think badly of her.

In person-centred therapy, trying to understand the client's inner world is fundamental and it may be very important to understand what a particular substance does – for instance, a client using heroin is likely to have been in considerable emotional (or physical) pain prior to using it. It is important for the counsellor to be aware of this and to tread gently and carefully in the client's inner world. Amphetamines, on the other hand, make the user feel wide awake and fully alive, and a client who particularly likes their effect may have a low-intensity fragile process that leaves them feeling deadened inside. Although some people do move from one substance (or excessive behaviour) to another, for others their chosen substance does a unique job and it may be important to appreciate just what it is that is so satisfying about that particular substance in order to understand their inner world more fully. Some knowledge about the general effects of a substance can be useful in understanding what using it, or not using it, may mean to the client.

The sixth condition – that the client perceives the counsellor as accept-ing and empathic – is something over which the counsellor has no control. A client will only feel safe enough to acknowledge the denied aspects of their organismic experience if they perceive the helper as unconditionally accepting and empathic. A client whose perception has been altered by the substance they have been using may well misunderstand the counsellor's attempts to convey the therapeutic conditions. Shame, anger, fear and low self-regard can also distort perception. There is nothing we can do to make a client perceive us as unconditionally accepting and empathic, but con-tinuing to remain so helps.

Jasmine

My face fell into a concerned frown as I listened to Jasmine, who had been using amphetamines very heavily indeed, speak about how her friends had been talking about her behind her back. She suddenly pulled her chair back and accused me of thinking that she was bad and of hating her as much as her friends did. I was surprised and assured her that this was not the case, but it took several sessions and no more amphetamines before she stopped suspecting me of thinking badly of her.

Conclusion

Alcohol and other drugs have, as everyone knows, very powerful effects. People who find themselves using a substance in excessive amounts over an excessively long period of time are not doing so because they feel a little uptight in social situations or because they like the taste or want to experiment with altered states of consciousness. For them it is not about adding a little zing to life but about making life bearable. People who find themselves dependent on alcohol or another drug are caught up in a nightmarish world in which the thing that makes life tolerable is simultaneously destroying it. The worse life gets, the more compulsive the substance becomes, and the only immediate reward in breaking this cycle may be frayed nerves and a life that is in tatters. Overcoming a chemical dependence is really difficult. A companion who is there no matter what, who does not judge or have expectations but who is genuine and does understand, can be of great help.

Guide to Further Reading

Bryant-Jefferies, R. (2001) *Counselling the Person Beyond the Alcohol Problem*. London: Jessica Kingsley.

Applies the principles of PCT practice to Prochaska and DiClemente's model (1982) of change with respect to addictive behaviour.

Farrell, M. (1996) 'A person-centred approach? "Working with addictions"', *Person Centred Practice*, 4 (1): 7–13.

Farrell discusses his struggle with the question of whether a person-centred approach is relevant and helpful in working for an organisation that provides a service for homeless people, many of whom drink very heavily.

Moerman, M. and McLeod, J. (2006) 'Person-centered counselling for alcohol-related problems: The client's experience of self in the therapeutic relationship', *Person-Centered & Experiential Therapies*, 5 (1): 21–35.

Moerman and McLeod use Inter-personal Process Recall and Grounded Theory to analyse the experience of clients of person-centred counselling for alcohol problems. Their findings show clients to be experience- rather than problem-focused.

Warner, M.S. (2000) 'Person-centred therapy at the difficult edge: A developmentally based model of fragile and dissociated process', in D. Mearns and B. Thorne (eds), *Person-Centred Therapy Today: New Frontiers in Theory and Practice*. London: Sage, pp. 144–171.

An introduction to the concepts of the fragile process and working with clients who find it difficult to moderate the intensity of their feelings.

Wilders, S. (2005) 'An exploration of non-directive work with drug and alcohol users', in B.E. Levitt (ed.), *Embracing Non-Directivity*. Ross-on-Wye: PCCS Books, pp. 192–202.

Advocates seeing clients who are under the influence of a substance, and argues that that not doing so fundamentally undermines the basic principles of PCT. Wilders discusses the unpredictable ways in which substances affect individuals and discusses working with someone who is incoherent.

References

Mearns, D. (2000) *Person-Centred Therapy Today*. London: Sage.

Mearns, D. and Thorne, B. (eds) (2000) *Person-Centred Therapy Today: New Frontiers in Theory and Practice*. London: Sage.

Prochaska, J.O. and DiClemente, C.C. (1982) 'Transtheoretical therapy: Towards a more integrative model of change', *Psychotherapy: Theory, Research and Practice*, 19: 276–88.

Rogers C.R. (1951) *Client-Centered Therapy*. London: Constable.

Rogers C.R. (1961) *On Becoming a Person: A Therapist's View of Psychotherapy*. London: Constable.

Warner M.S. (2000) 'Person-centred therapy at the difficult edge: A developmentally based model of fragile and dissociated process', in D. Mearns and B. Thorne (eds), *Person-Centred Therapy Today: New Frontiers in Theory and Practice*. London: Sage, pp. 144–171.

9

WORKING WITH CLIENTS WHO HAVE EATING PROBLEMS

BARBARA DOUGLAS

Introduction: What are Eating Difficulties?

In this chapter I outline some pertinent issues for the person-centred therapist in working with clients who are experiencing eating difficulties. I explore some person-centred concepts as they relate to therapeutic work and illustrate these through case vignettes indicating processes of change and therapy.

From the point of view of those who do not suffer them, eating disorders are generally considered to include anorexia, bulimia and binge eating disorder. In terms of a medical model, there is also a category called 'eating disorders not otherwise specified' – usually referred to as EDNOS. Generally, eating disorders are regarded as a response to a combination of factors rather than as having a single cause. The repertoire of causes may include low self-esteem, family relationship issues, loss, problems with study or work, bullying or abuse. They may occur when food is used to cope with feelings such as anxiety, anger, loneliness, inadequacy, boredom, shame, failure, loss of control or sadness. In addition there is evidence of biological predisposition in some people (Bulik et al., 2000).

Specialist services for people with eating problems have emerged, albeit geographically patchily, across the United Kingdom, and can be found within both the national health and private sectors. From a therapist perspective, clients with eating problems are sometimes perceived as difficult, intransigent and manipulative, with relatively poor outcome prospects. However, intransigence, resistance and manipulation may be understood as challenging the way that 'outsiders' (doctors, therapists and other professionals) see the problem of 'eating disorders'. From the client perspective, there are as many meanings to eating difficulties as there are clients who experience them.

Many clients refer to their eating difficulty, be it anorexia, bulimia or binge eating, as being like an addiction. Others see their relationship with food and weight as an identity, so much a part of themselves that without it they can see no person in themselves. Fear encompasses much of the experience of relating to food: fear of losing an identity, of being a non-person, of losing control or of being without means of existing in the world. This level of fear can result in an all-encompassing passion for daily weight-loss and food control that may be heavily defended from anyone perceived as attempting to subvert it.

Just as the nature, causes and experiences of eating problems are numerous and complex, so are there also many models put forward to offer frameworks for understanding these responses to distress. These include:

- Biomedical models that focus on a genetic predisposition to eating problems and/or links between 'abnormal' brain chemistry and behaviour (see, for example, Kaye et al., 2005).
- Psychosocial models that consider eating problems as a means of dealing with low self-esteem emerging from personal, familial and cultural experiences such as adverse childhood experiences or the impact of bullying (see, for example, Womble et al., 2001).
- Social constructionist models that consider the concept of disorder itself as historical, cultural and/or gendered, asking, for example, why we have constructed a disorder that emphasises a drive for thinness rather than a drive for muscularity (see, for example, McVittie et al., 2005).

Research to date therefore suggests the adoption of a biopsychosocial model that integrates the many factors included in the models above. Yet whichever model is emphasised in understanding eating problems, these behavioural responses cause immense distress both to the individual experiencing them and to those around them. In 2004, the National Institute for Health and Clinical Excellence (NICE) estimated that, in the UK, 1 in 200 females and 1 in 2000 males will suffer from anorexia, which also has the highest mortality rate of any of the psychiatric classifications of eating problems or all psychiatric classifications. Five times as many people suffer from bulimia, and, in addition, long-term problems are not uncommon in people experiencing either or both.

The Process of Change

Based on research evidence, Rogers concluded that, in the facilitation of constructive personality change, 'it is the attitude and feelings of

the therapist – rather than his theoretical orientation – which is important' (Rogers, 1961: 44). In focusing on the attitudes of the therapist
and offering the therapist-provided conditions, a person-centred
therapist will seek to be accurately attuned to the client's own process
of change – so facilitating the client's actualising tendency towards
fluidity of experience of self and others (see **Chapter 1**). This is
a central platform on which to turn to the process of therapy and
how the person-centred therapist might engage with some of the tensions and issues inherent in working with clients who have eating
problems.

Beginning

Assessment is a debated and even contentious concept amongst person-
centred therapists. When we meet a new client we inevitably engage
with them in an enquiring way, and Wilkins' (2005: 141–3) model of
process rather than pathology in assessment is a helpful one in working
with clients with eating problems. By asking whether with a particular
client the six conditions can be present, going forward with therapy
becomes a decision based as much on the therapist as the client. It is
concerned with the interactional space between them where the psychological meeting that facilitates the actualising tendency may take
place. When working with clients with an eating difficulty, the therapist needs to ask:

- Can we establish psychological contact?
- Does this client want and need therapy?
- Can I offer this client the therapist-provided conditions?
- Can they experience my empathy and unconditional positive regard?

Therapists working with this client group can find themselves working
at the edges of therapy (and, on occasion, life itself). The client who is
both vomiting and taking laxatives regularly is at serious risk of elec-
trolyte imbalance and depletions that in the case of potassium deficiency may cause sudden death from heart irregularities. Equally, the
teenage diabetic client who is binge eating is in danger of slipping into
a coma or of suffering from retinopathy (a serious eye disease resulting
in blindness), and the emaciated client who appears energetic may
develop rapid organ failure. Therapists have a responsibility to consider
their own position within this and how this affects the work that they
are able to undertake with such clients. If we adopt Wilkins' assessment
of process model it becomes apparent that in some instances we may
appropriately decide that we cannot work with a client. The following
vignette offers an illustration.

Ben

Ben was referred to the eating disorders service by his GP. The referral letter stated that Ben had refused inpatient treatment and asked that the outpatient service see him. On opening the door to him I was shocked by the extent to which he was visibly emaciated. During the hour we spent together, my level of anxiety about his continued survival made a therapeutic relationship impossible for me. I had a deep sense of attendant possible harm to the client in a setting where medical intervention was not readily accessible. Although Carrick (2007) outlines the opportunity for change that can be encapsulated in the notion of crisis, in this instance while I understood Ben's fears of inpatient treatment, I concluded that I would be unable to work with him and conveyed this to Ben. This was not an easy process for me because it challenged my belief in the individual's intuitive knowledge of what is best for them. Yet, that same sense is part of my own process and I was aware of an inherent trust in my course of action in this instance. Ben and I discussed a letter to his GP outlining why we would not be proceeding.

As the above vignette also indicates, clients and therapists always work within some broader context that is likely to have a bearing on the ability of the therapist to offer the therapist-provided conditions. For example, clients may self-refer or be referred; see the therapist independently or as part of a multidisciplinary service; or have been encouraged by others to seek help or have come to that decision themselves. So too there may be considerable variance in the ability of specific organisations to facilitate the safe development of a therapeutic space that enables work at relational depth.

For example, the client may have chosen to see a private therapist specifically because they do not want their eating difficulties noted on their medical record. At the initial meeting, however, if the therapist is anxiously wondering whether their client's swollen purple toes are indications that the client is at serious physical risk, they need to be in a position to work within their competence, as well as to address the anxiety that will impact on their congruence. Thus if the client/therapist dyad is to be adequately supported with respect to the physical issues that are attendant on eating problems, the therapist working independently may want to include the possibility of both therapist and client communication with the GP practice as part of a contract to work together.

At initial meetings with other clients these issues may not arise, and, indeed, some clients with eating difficulties experience feelings of being undeserving of help precisely because they are *not* in an extreme physical condition. Unwarranted emphasis on the dramatic ends of eating difficulties can in some instances confirm this response. The following vignette illustrates the need for empathic attunement to the client's process at the initial meeting.

Jenny

Jenny was seventeen when she was referred to the eating disorders service by her GP. She was reluctant to attend the service and had come in order to please her mother, who was extremely worried about her loss of weight and isolation from friends. Jenny stated that her weight was not a problem for her and that she felt better about herself when she was empty.

When Jenny understood that I was not going to try to make her eat, she began to relax a bit and talked about her teenage years. She described a pervasive feeling that there was something wrong with her, something that made her different from her peers. She described being an overweight child and told me that when she was thirteen, she developed glandular fever and was off school for several weeks. During this period she lost some weight and noticed that she felt a sense of pleasure at this. On returning to school she discovered that the hockey team had been chosen in her absence and so the sport that she loved was no longer open to her. Her friendship group seemed to have realigned too and she felt excluded. Jenny increasingly withdrew into herself and her schoolwork, becoming the target of a group of girls who taunted her. Jenny remembered the good feeling she had when she had lost weight and thought that if she cut down a bit things might get better and the taunting might stop. Concentrating on her weight loss gave Jenny a sense of being good at something. But her family, she said, were now watching her to see what she was eating, trying to put high-fat things into her food when they thought that she was not looking. Her parents frequently argued about her eating and her sister just said that she wanted the old Jenny back. Jenny cried when saying that she knew that it was all her fault, she was the cause of the problems and there was something inherently wrong with her.

Towards the end of the session I asked Jenny whether she wanted to come back next week. She said that she was surprised that talking about all this had been a relief. She had only come, she said, to get her mother off her back but actually she would like to come back next week.

Although this was only the beginning of a long and sometimes very bumpy road towards a more comfortable way of living for Jenny, it is used here to illustrate the importance of being empathically attuned to where in the process of change a client is when they enter the therapy room. Despite her being underweight, to have adopted an approach that sought behavioural change of Jenny at that point would have very likely have led to her withdrawing from the process there and then. As it was, she experienced what it felt like to be able to communicate some of her distress and for that simply to be heard with no expectations.

Assessing whether client and therapist are able to make psychological contact is also relevant to the initial meeting with clients with eating problems. People who are severely emaciated with anorexia, for example, are often experienced as being unable to engage in psychological therapy because of their extreme black-and-white thinking, remoteness and determination to self-sufficiency. Alternatively the client with bulimia will often have been prescribed a high dose of an antidepressant prior to referral to therapy. Although there is some evidence that drugs such as fluoxetine reduce the number of episodes of bingeing and vomiting, one of the other effects can be an emotional distancing from feelings such that experience may be blunted. I can only pose the question of whether psychological contact is a prerequisite and hampered by such effects or whether the therapist might be able to facilitate the development of psychological contact by trusting in the process of a relationship, however tenuous to begin with, in ameliorating such difficulties to a point where psychological contact can emerge. Considering whether psychological contact can be experienced and maintained by therapist and client is, however, clearly of some importance in the decisions made by therapist and client as to whether to work together. Although it is beyond the scope of this chapter to consider in detail, there are in fact established person-centred strategies, such as those used in pre-therapy, for creating and strengthening psychological contact (see, for example, Sanders, 2007). These may be useful if there appears to be a challenge to contact.

Ongoing work

The self-structure

Rogers suggested that incongruence results from internalised conditions of worth that create a greater reliance on external locus of value than an internal valuing process. For example, the client with binge eating problems who experienced her own and her sister's family place in terms of 'she was the pretty one and I was the clever one' may have developed an intense need to achieve straight A grades at school. Sustained bullying experienced in early adolescence is something that is frequently reported by clients with an eating problem and has been found to have major consequences for mental health (Schreier et al., 2009). It may engender a developing sense of the self as deeply unworthy or as in Jenny's experience, as 'something wrong with me'. In this way relationships with others become perceived through the lens of such a distorted self concept, being viewed as any or all of being threatening, unreliable, untrustworthy or inconsistent. Anorexia, bulimia or binge eating, by contrast, far from being experienced as a problem, initially appear to offer ways of having a 'reliable' relationship, where food or its control is experienced as a friend, as a reliable solution.

Thus, an empathically attuned therapeutic relationship, rather than a symptom-orientated approach alone, is a vital factor in the client's emerging experience of self as of intrinsic worth and developing ability to trust in their own internal locus of evaluation. In this way the therapeutic relationship facilitates the person's movement towards a more comfortable self-structure experience of relationships with people and reduction in the need to rely on an all-important relationship with food.

Configurations of self

Specific behavioural responses to distress reflect multiple dimensions of existence or configurations of self. Campling (2007: 23–4), for example, describes his own experience of anorexia as the dominance of an 'anorexic self'. Equally, the notion of the eating problem as 'friend', so often described by those seeking help, acts as another, externalised, aspect of the self. Such configurations may be at the edge of awareness, and clients will offer them in a variety of ways, as for example in the statement, 'I wouldn't know who I am without the anorexia.'

It follows therefore that change will also have multiple meanings for the client, which may include a profound fear of existential loss as well as the hoped-for relief from distress. This is reflected in the many ups and downs of what is often long-term work with clients with eating problems. Frustration is sometimes experienced at the clients' lack of progress but may result from the therapist remaining within their own frame of reference from where it is hard to hear these multiple meanings of change. For example, clients with eating disorders may express feelings of being undeserving. After all, they argue, they are being offered help when a part of them does not want to get better, even if they do want the misery to stop. The vignette below illustrates the powerful nature of sharing configurations of self.

Working with the parts

James

James was a twenty-two-year-old man who attended an open group for people with eating problems. James' previous inpatient treatment for anorexia had restored him to normal weight but on discharge he quickly began to lose weight again. In the open group he shared his hopes that talking to others experiencing similar difficulties might be helpful. After about forty minutes, James, with eyes to the floor, whispered: 'I know that I am a fraud really because 2 per cent of me wants to get better but 98 per cent does not, so I don't really know why I am here, how you can help me or even if I want help.' The experienced impact of his honesty within the group was evidenced visibly and vocally, stimulating animated discussion of how others experienced these feelings too and perhaps did not need to feel so 'bad' if they were shared by others.

One of the most visibly powerful moments of change happens when in therapy we acknowledge that all parts of a person can be heard. I guess that this particular young man was there because he wanted to hold onto and grow the 2 per cent part that was in that moment being symbolised. To do this it was also important to him that his feelings of shame and being undeserving were heard as another important part of his process.

Symbolisation

Just as James described parts of himself in terms of percentages, so images are regularly introduced by clients as symbolisations of aspects of self. Vehicles, either static or racing out of control, weeds that grow within the brain or monsters within the body are but a few. In the vignette below, Jasminder brings the imagery of a computer to convey her sense of experience in relation to others. Being in the symbolisation together or, at a later stage of symbolisation, talking about the imagery, can be experienced by client and therapist as deeply meaningful and a powerful process in developing a personal sense of meaning. Mearns and Thorne (2000: 128) suggest that to attempt actively to change the client's symbolisation is to interfere with their fundamental process and, if their locus of evaluation is external, may be actively damaging. The vividness of the imagery can lead to a sense of wanting to develop it, to 'move the client on', and yet in experiencing such a desire it is perhaps important that we ask ourselves why and whose need this is. In their symbolisation of self the client may take the imagery development in their own direction if facilitated rather than directed.

> **Jasminder**
>
> Jasminder was twenty-four years old when she was referred to me by her GP. She had experienced anorexia in her teens and, following the sudden and unexpected death of her close friend earlier in the year, her eating behaviours returned. During one session, Jasminder told me about how she had switched on the computer earlier in the week to find a message on the screen stating that because of a problem the computer was in 'safe mode' in order to protect its functions. Jasminder animatedly told me that this was exactly how she felt; she was in safe mode and the anorexia gave her a means to retain that sense of safety, a sense of being in control. This metaphor represented a powerful point of change for Jasminder. It made coherent sense to her that her eating problem was simultaneously both protector and trapper. In addition, for Jasminder, the sense of 'protector' that came into her awareness enabled her to begin to see herself in a more accepting light with regard to her struggle with change.

Holding experience in attention

Within early care-giving relationships where empathic attunement has been either unavailable or unpredictable, the development of the child's ability to self-soothe in the face of experienced over-arousal is either absent or disrupted. In person-centred terms, holding experience in attention may be felt as intolerable. Margaret Warner (2000: 149) states that:

> Children may never develop a capacity to hold experience in attention to check the felt rightness of its meaning. Their personal senses of experiential recognition, or the lack of it, may be unattended to or actively avoided and disparaged.

Eating difficulties are sometimes considered as behavioural solutions for the moderation of arousal in the absence of more comfortable means of self-soothing because they frequently act, at least initially, to dampen the edges of experience. The numbing of emotions in binge eating, the detachedness of the felt experience in anorexia, or the anaesthesia of feeling in an episode of bulimia can all reliably and predictably be brought into play to dull an intensity of feeling that threatens to overwhelm. As Warner (2000: 100) reflects, 'the body offers a lived way of responding to the person's whole situation'.

Thus, just as the child's ability to self-soothe is disrupted, so too does the vulnerable emerging adult find in an eating problem an approximation to this process that temporarily quietens body and mind. However, because it leaves the individual unnourished, there emerges a resultant and increasing internal incongruence, one that does not remain static but burgeons into experiences that are likened to addiction and an increasing sense of being trapped. This may well be a point at which help is sought as the person attempts to make sense of what is happening to them.

Fragile process

Clients with eating problems tend to be pathologised, often with 'co-morbid' disorder-specific labels such as borderline personality disorder, dissociative disorder or obsessive compulsive disorder. Warner (2005: 98–9), however, makes a compelling argument for regarding such behaviours and experiences as forms of difficult processing of meaning:

> Processing – a particular sort of self directed, individual way of making sense of life experience in the context of human relationships – is a central aspect of the way human beings are adapted to function as human beings. ... one would expect people to keep trying to process, even under conditions of severe challenge. Any significant inability to process would tend to be experienced as affliction and to cause severe dysfunction in a person's ability to live effectively among other human beings.

In eating problems, some of these ways of processing are made visible. A client with anorexia may experience a dissociated process of meaning-making in which an inner and relational sense of emptiness and disconnectedness is replaced by intense engagement in relationship with food and weight that offers a powerful sense of purpose. A client with bulimia may experience a fragile process in which the experience of intense emotion without effective means of self-soothing can at least temporarily be ameliorated through vomiting or purging.

In addition, self-harm, which is sometimes associated with eating problems, acts to reduce psychological distress by replacing it with a focus on bodily experience. 'I feel calm when I cut myself' is something not infrequently reported. A dissociated form of processing meaning may also be mirrored in the act of binge eating, which is sometimes described as losing awareness of oneself in a period of driven food intake. Dissociated processing, as sometimes manifested in eating problems, may also be a consequence of intolerable childhood traumatic experience in which there was no available means of coping beyond switching off the ability to hold awareness in experience, as, for example, in sexual abuse (Hawkins, 2007).

Coming to sense and listen to one's own experiencing self in the presence of a facilitative, authentic and predictable relationship with a therapist represents a movement to trust in self and other rather than the objects of food and weight. In the presence of a predictable prizing relationship, the client develops their ability to self-soothe, to author a coherent narrative meaning of themselves and their relationships in the world. Therefore it makes sense that the therapist's adoption of an expert stance, while perhaps initially comforting to a client in distress, is unlikely to offer a relationship in which the client can develop their own expertness, or as Warner puts it, 'to integrate clusters of experience in ways that carry forward the whole organism' (Warner, 2005: 102).

Behavioural experimentation

Non-directivity in the person-centred approach is a debated construct (Wilkins, 2003: 90; Gillon, 2007: 13–15), and Mearns and Thorne (2000: 191) suggest that we consider it as functional rather than structural: 'the importance of directivity is not in what the counsellor *does* but in what the client *experiences*'. Similarly, Grant (2002) argues that 'instrumental non-directivity' can be as much "technique driven" as directive action and distinguishes it in this sense from 'principled non directivity', which refers to an attitude of non-interference. Thus, notions such as moving a client into the next stage of a process of change would be antithetical. Equally, however, Campling (2007) suggests that having some knowledge and not sharing it could be considered incongruent. Although condition-specific service provision may have conceptual difficulties from a person-centred perspective, it does provide an opportunity for the therapist to build a personal resource of what can be experienced as helpful – something that perhaps reflects the client's own process in therapy.

Certainly, the process of many clients with eating difficulties is likely to include a felt need to address the powerful sense of addiction, whether this is to starvation or binge eating, with or without vomiting. Food diaries, structured with headings that enable the client to examine and rate patterns of thoughts and feelings related to eating behaviours are frequently used across approaches to eating problems in order to address this point. The potential usefulness of keeping a food diary may be brought to the client's attention by the person-centred therapist simply as an available resource, 'something that may be helpful to some people, and if you are interested we can explore the use of these'. Alternatively, drawing a 'ladder of fear' in which foods are placed according to how fearfully they are experienced may be a way of experimenting gradually with the client's desired change. The therapist is a resource for possibilities but the client is the driver of what, if anything, resonates with them. The client's internal locus of evaluation has primacy. Such 'behavioural experiments' are usually only one part of the client's process of change but nevertheless one that may be important, as is illustrated in the vignette below.

Deborah

Deborah was a mother of three young daughters when she was referred to the service. She was significantly underweight, her periods had stopped and she maintained a ritualistic pattern of eating that restricted her to tiny amounts of a few foods at specific times of day. She felt overwhelmed at the care of three children under five years of age but was also scared of passing her food fears onto her daughters. Deborah specifically wanted help to change her eating patterns and we discussed the use of a food diary, which Deborah was keen to try. During the session, we worked through its structure and aims, using an example from Deborah's most recent experience to complete the form. Deborah took copies home to complete and bring back the following week for us to discuss. Deborah was encouraged when she discovered patterns of situations, thoughts and feelings that she experienced as linked to her eating behaviour, although she struggled to make changes. One week, however, she came in saying that rather than completing the structured forms, she found it helpful to use the blank side of the form to write down how she felt immediately after eating as this gave her a way of coping with her increased anxiety following eating until it had subsided. The forms continued to be important to Deborah over the following weeks and, rather than writing on blank paper, she continued to ask for the forms and to use the blank side to aid her in becoming more comfortable around food. In this way, the suggestion of food diaries had been helpful to Deborah in making the changes that she wanted, but she had taken it forward in her own fashion, experimenting in approaches that she experienced as helpful to her.

Ending

How much is enough?

The idea that a client begins therapy with an eating disorder and ends without it may be how both therapist and client would ideally like to see the therapeutic process. While for Jasminder in the earlier vignette above, the ending naturally reflected her developing internal locus of evaluation, this 'ideal' ending is by no means always the case (and we also need to ask whose 'ideal' when using this word). For various reasons, outlined below, the therapeutic relationship is likely to be only a part of the client's route towards finding a more comfortable way of being in the world. For example, many clients with eating problems are young people whose external lives are in a relatively fluid process of change (something that may itself be part of the experienced difficulty). A move from school to sixth form college can mean necessary changes to appointment times that may or may not be possible to accommodate. Alternatively, leaving the area to begin university elsewhere may bring therapy to a close, as may leaving university to begin work. Equally, establishing a relationship with a new partner may lead to feelings of well-being such that the client no longer feels a need to attend therapy. Clients may leave because they do not find therapy helpful or they may want to explore only part of their process within therapy. For example, the client who is vomiting twice daily at the beginning of therapy and reduces this to once a week may experience this as good enough. As therapists, we might experience this as less than (our) ideal – yet this is our disappointment. We may be failing to recognise and trust the client's intuitive understanding of their needs within their own fragile process or perhaps that a reduction in the need for perfection in all aspects of their life is something that the client values.

Service issues also impact on endings. Session numbers in the organisational context of the NHS, for example, are as likely to relate to the structure and nature of service provision, NICE guidelines and the waiting list rather than the individual needs of the particular client. Yet the client will likely experience these limits personally in terms of their own conditions of worth and self-structure, perhaps as an 'expert' indication of when they should be 'better' or as a means of 'getting rid' of them. Pragmatically, however, limitations exist and will continue to exist within organisational contexts, and the client has a right to expect that we will respect their sense of what are safe or unsafe frameworks within which they can work. Clients with fragile process who experience themselves as very needy and dependent may know at some level that their process of change cannot be facilitated within the NICE guideline service provision of sixteen to twenty sessions, and so they decide not to return after the initial meeting. The therapist who encourages such a client to return may be confirming the client's view that they cannot trust their experiential self or alternatively may find themselves and their client in a mess of abandonment experiences further down the line because neither was listening to the client's internal sense at the beginning.

'How much is enough?' is a question many people struggling with eating problems ask about food at some point during therapy. The question can also be asked of the therapeutic process. 'How much therapy is enough?' is a question regularly answered by a combination of the client's experiential trusting of their process, the therapist's empathic attunement and factors that resonate with external world events.

Conclusion

I have written this chapter from a stance that takes account of both client and research knowledge but in which attitudes and a way of being with self and client are fundamental to the process of change. As far as is possible within the constraints of a single chapter, I have explored some of the issues that may emerge during the therapeutic process, and trust that I have given something of the flavour of working where eating difficulties are part of the client's world.

Guide to Further Reading

Campling, M. (2007) 'A person-centred response to eating disorders: A personal experience', in R. Worsley and S. Joseph (eds), *Person-Centred Practice: Case Studies in Positive Psychology*. Ross-on-Wye: PCCS Books, pp. 21–30.

This is an account of the experience of having an eating disorder. It is helpful too in that it goes some way to dispelling the notion that only women and girls experience difficulties with food.

Marchant, L. and Payne, H. (2002) 'The experience of counselling for female clients with anorexia nervosa: A person-centred perspective', *Counselling and Psychotherapy Research*, 2 (2): 127–32.

The purpose of this study is to understand the experiences of clients who had received counselling for anorexia nervosa, and to set these experiences against the backdrop of person-centred theory. The study is based on an intensive heuristic analysis of interviews with five clients who had completed counselling for anorexia nervosa within the previous three months. Collaboration between the researcher and the participants led to an identification of two of the six 'core' conditions identified by Rogers as being of real importance to clients with anorexia: unconditional positive regard and congruence. The context in which counselling is offered was also of crucial significance to these clients.

Worsley, R. (2005) 'Small-scale research as personal development for mental health professionals', in S. Joseph and R. Worsley (eds), *Person-Centred Psychopathology: A Positive Psychology of Mental Health*. Ross-on-Wye: PCCS Books, pp. 337–47.

Although the focus of this chapter is on research processes it may be helpful when beginning to work with people who have difficulties with food because it is an account of how the writer addressed his discomfort at working with people with anorexia.

As well as the above texts, readers may find papers, chapters and books listed in the **References** section below helpful in expanding their understanding of person-centred approaches to difficulties with food.

References

Bulik, C., Sullivan, P., Wade, T. and Kendler, K. (2000) 'Twin studies of eating disorders: A review', *International Journal of Eating Disorders*, 27: 1–20.

Campling, M. (2007) 'A person-centred response to eating disorders: A personal experience', in R. Worsley and S. Joseph (eds), *Person-Centred*

Practice: Case Studies in Positive Psychology. Ross-on-Wye: PCCS Books, pp. 21–30.

Carrick, L. (2007) 'Crisis intervention', in M. Cooper, M. O'Hara, P. Schnid and G. Wyatt (eds), *The Handbook of Person-Centred Psychotherapy and Counselling*. Basingstoke: Palgrave, pp. 293–304.

Gillon, E. (2007) *Person-Centred Counselling Psychology: An Introduction*. London: Sage.

Grant, B. (2002) 'Principled and instrumental non-directiveness in person-centred and client-centred therapy', in D.J. Cain (ed.), *Classics in the Person-Centred Approach*. Ross on Wye: PCCS Books, pp. 371–7.

Hawkins, J. (2007) 'Recovering from childhood sexual abuse: Dissociative processing', in R. Worsley and S. Joseph (eds), *Person-Centred Practice: Case Studies in Positive Psychology*. Ross-on-Wye: PCCS Books, pp. 85–97.

Kaye, W., Frank, G., Bailer, U. and Henry, S. (2005) 'Neurobiology of anorexia nervosa: Clinical implications of alterations of the function of serotonin and other neuronal systems', *International Journal of Eating Disorders*, 37: 515–19.

McVittie, C., Cavers, D. and Hepworth, J. (2005) 'Femininity, mental weakness and difference: Male students account for anorexia nervosa in men', *Sex Roles*, 53 (5): 413–41.

Mearns, D. and Thorne, B. (eds) (2000) *Person-Centred Therapy Today: New Frontiers in Theory and Practice*. London: Sage.

Rogers, C.R. (1961) *On Becoming a Person: A Therapist's View of Psychotherapy*. London: Constable.

Sanders, P. (ed.) (2007) *The Contact Work Primer*. Ross-on-Wye: PCCS Books.

Schreier, A., Wolke, D. and Thomas, K. (2009) 'Prospective study of peer victimization in childhood and psychotic symptoms in a nonclinical population at age 12 years', *Archives of General Psychiatry*, 66: 527–36.

Warner, M.S. (2000) 'Person-centred therapy at the difficult edge: A developmentally based model of fragile and dissociated process', in D. Mearns and B. Thorne (eds), *Person-Centred Therapy Today: New Frontiers in Theory and Practice*. London: Sage, pp. 144–71.

Warner, M.S. (2005) 'A person-centred view of human nature, wellness and psychopathology', in S. Joseph and R. Worsley (eds), *Person-Centred Psychopathology: A Positive Psychology of Mental Health*. Ross-on-Wye: PCCS Books, pp. 91–109.

Wilkins, P. (2003) *Person-Centred Therapy in Focus*. London: Sage.

Wilkins, P. (2005) 'Assessment and diagnosis in person-centred therapy', in S. Joseph and R. Worsley (eds), *Person-Centred Psychopathology: A Positive Psychology of Mental Health*. Ross-on-Wye: PCCS Books, pp. 128–45.

Womble, L.G., Williamson, D.A., Martin, C.K., Zucker, N.L., Thaw, J.M., Netemeyer, R., Lovejoy, J. and Greenway, F. (2001) 'Psychosocial variables associated with binge eating in obese males and females', *International Journal of Eating Disorders*, 30 (2): 217–21.

10

A PERSON-CENTRED PERSPECTIVE ON SELF-INJURY

ROSE CAMERON

for Yehmanja 1992–2009

NOTE: Although the term 'self-harm' is more commonly used in Britain, I will be using the term 'self-injury' in order to make a distinction between deliberate self-wounding and other forms of harmful behaviour discussed in other chapters of this book.

Introduction: Why Do People Self-Injure?

> Most people who saw my injuries reacted with scorn or disgust. They saw cutting as a sign of weakness, juvenile attention-seeking. I, on the other hand, viewed it as a logical means of dealing with the emotional chaos within me, allowing me to function on a day-to-day basis. (Anonymous, *Guardian Weekend*, 30 September 2006: 12)

It is common, both in the literature and in specialist help, for self-injury to be spoken of in the same breath as attempted suicide. The two, however, are different. Someone who cuts deeply into their wrists is trying to die. Someone who makes superficial cuts to their arms and legs is not. Someone who sets themselves alight is trying to die; someone who deliberately burns themselves with a cigarette is trying to do something else. Biting or punching oneself is not potentially lethal, nor is pulling out hair, breaking bones, preventing wounds from healing or swallowing indigestible objects. Although many people who self-harm often feel suicidal, the relationship between the two is much more complex than that of a half-hearted suicide attempt.

Specialist services tend to view self-inflicted injury in terms of behaviour rather than motivation, and may make little or no distinction between those who intend to die and those who do not. People who self-harm often describe their self-injury as a means of *preventing* suicide, and express huge frustration at their behaviour being misunderstood as a desire to die rather than to live. The belief amongst many professionals that self-injury is on a continuum with suicide results in both overreaction and under-reaction. Depending on the severity of their injuries, someone who has deliberately harmed themselves is as likely to be dismissed as 'attention seeking' as they are to be sectioned.

Having emphasised the difference between self-injury and attempted suicide, I want to acknowledge that a small number of people, usually those who injure themselves whilst dissociated or for whom self-injury is not having the desired effect, do injure themselves in a way that is life threatening. I also want to acknowledge how disturbing it can be to see or hear about self-injury. Wanting your client to stop is a very understandable response, but it may not be a helpful one.

So, in instances in which self-injury is not about wanting to die, what is it about? Much of the professional literature on the subject comes from psychiatry and psychology. When not equating it with attempted suicide, this literature is mostly about borderline personality disorder, although self-injury is also associated with mood disorders, eating disorders, obsessive-compulsive disorders, post-traumatic stress disorder, dissociative disorders and anxiety disorders. When it is not considered to be a symptom of any of these disorders, self-injury is sometimes considered a disorder in itself (Favazza and Rosenthal, 1993; Favazza, 1996; Alderman, 1997).

Most of the self-help literature discusses self-injury in terms of a 'disorder' or 'addiction' and is almost invariably written from a cognitive-behavioural perspective (as most self-help guides are – relationally based approaches like the person-centred approach do not easily lend themselves to a 'do it alone' treatment). There are a number of autobiographical accounts of self-harm, and these also tend to be about how the author 'overcame' or 'healed from' their 'disorder' or 'addiction'.

Professional literature by and for counsellors and psychotherapists on the subject of self-harm is surprisingly sparse although Maggie Turp's *Hidden Self-Harm* gives an accessible psychoanalytic perspective. However, there seems to be no consideration, from a person-centred view as to why some people deliberately injure themselves. Person-centred theory insists that such behaviour must not only be purposeful and goal directed but also be part of an overall tendency to self-regulation, maintenance and growth. I argue that indeed it is, and that deliberate self-injury illustrates how effectively the organism finds a precise solution to a particular challenge.

A Person-Centred Perspective on Self-Injury

There is nothing immediately obvious in PCT theory that would explain why punching one's self in the face or eating a lightbulb is a manifestation of the actualising tendency. However, a person-centred approach would suggest that listening to those who do such things to themselves would be a good way to start developing some accurate understanding. People who self-harm give many different reasons for doing so. These include:

- I burn myself because I am bad, and deserve to suffer. That may sound ridiculous, and a lot of people have told me it is, but if you knew what I know, you would see that it is right.
- I do it because I hurt inside. It helps to see it.
- I do it when I am annoyed with my boyfriend or my mum. I know it makes them feel sorry.
- I do it when I feel really bad because everyone is ignoring how I feel.
- I'm frightened that if I didn't punch myself, I'd punch one of the kids.
- I don't really know why I do it.
- I hurt myself when I am angry. I don't really know why, but it makes me feel better.
- Seeing the blood come out makes me feel less stressed.
- It makes me feel alive and I start to feel a part of things again. I know that sounds weird, but it's how it is.
- Hurting myself takes my mind off the pain inside. Burning myself is good because it hurts for ages afterwards.
- I need that feeling of being in control.
- I don't know why, but I can think better when I'm going through a period of hurting myself. Everything just seems to be clearer, and I seem to react quicker to things and make better decisions. I have a job with lots of responsibilities, and sometimes I just feel like I'm losing the plot. If I go back to cutting, it just seems to help ... a lot. I sort of wish it didn't 'cos then I could stop, but I'm really glad it does, otherwise I don't know what I'd do.
- When I cut myself, I feel a lot calmer and I cope with things better. Sometimes, when I'm trying not to do it, things get really bad, and I've tried to kill myself a couple of times. I never get to that point when I am cutting, but I have to do it an awful lot.
- It calms me down.

Clearly the motivation for self-injury varies hugely from individual to individual. Some people don't know why they do it, but although they may not have a cognitive understanding of why they deliberately injure themselves, doing so makes sense to them at some level.

Self-Injury as Self-Regulation

Having conveyed something of the number and complexity of motivations for self-injury, I will now drastically simplify matters and say that most people self-injure in order to change the intensity of their psychological experience. Although the reasons above look varied, they can all be understood as ways of altering psychological tension. Some people do this by using self-injury to express how they feel. This reduces internal pressure by making an internal feeling external – 'getting it out'. People who use self-harm in this way do not necessarily show their wounds to anyone else. Like the person who said, *'I do it because I hurt inside. It helps to see it'*, they may find that giving their internal feeling external expression is helpful in itself.

Clients who do show their wounds to others or injure themselves in someone else's presence, or say things like, *'I do it when I feel really bad because everyone is ignoring how I feel'* are often seen as 'attention seeking' and 'manipulative'. They are, of course. We all manipulate those around us to some degree in order to try to meet our needs, and the need for contact and attention is a basic human trait. We all use our interactions with other people to affect the intensity of our feelings. Counselling is a very specialised way of doing this, but ideally many of our relationships help us cope with difficult feelings and savour the good. As with counselling, making contact or getting someone's attention is a precondition to any other form of relating. Although research (Suyemoto, 1998) shows that those who self-harm in order to get attention are in the minority, some people do say that they self-injure for this reason, and the fact that they are taking such desperate measures to make contact suggests that they are experiencing desperate need.

Some people talk about self-injury giving them a sense of control over themselves and what is happening to them. Whilst some of these people are in situations in which they feel controlled by someone else, not all are. Self-injury enables a lot of people to gain control of their own psychological state. The idea of controlling one's psychological state does not go down well with many a person-centred therapist, so it is important to recognise that we all control or, to use more therapy-friendly language, 'regulate' our feelings. We use internal resources such as breathing deeply when anxious and external resources such as seeking an apology when we are angry. As we saw above, even simply expressing our feelings can be a way of regulating the degree of psychological tension that we are experiencing. Being heard and empathically understood helps us regulate our feelings further – they may become more intense for a period of time as we feel more able to experience them fully, but then they generally become less intense and we 'move on' to our next experience.

Those who are not able to use the resources of adequately accepting and empathic relationships may dissociate or 'cut off' in order to reduce the intensity of what they are feeling. Many people do not experience the process of dissociation as voluntary and some people's brains have developed in such a way that it leaves them no option other than dissociation when stressed (Schore, 2003a). Many, like the person who said that they self-injured because *'it makes me feel alive and I start to feel a part of things again'*, use self-injury in order to end a period of dissociation. Using self-injury in order to *initiate* a period of dissociation seems to be much less common, but some people do use it in this way.

It is not difficult to understand empathically that injuring oneself can facilitate dissociation, as dissociating, or 'numbing', is a common response to any injury. Nor is it difficult to imagine that, conversely, the physical pain of an injury might bring someone 'back to their senses'. I imagine that most counsellors could also empathically understand a client who sheds tears of blood or wore their wounds on the outside. However, many people who self-harm distinguish 'calming down' from both self-expression and dissociation. It seems that deliberate self-injury has some kind of stress-reducing effect, whether or not it also serves an expressive or dissociate function.

'Reducing tension' or 'calming down' was the most widely cited reason across a variety of client groups in a meta study into why people deliberately injure themselves (Klonsky, 2007). This can be, for those who do not self-injure, the most difficult to understand empathically. Injury *causes* tension for most people – we wince and brace ourselves against the pain. People who deliberately injure themselves in order to release tension have the opposite response – they relax and wind down. Subjects in a piece of research into self-injury (Haines et al., 1995) were asked to imagine harming themselves. Those in the group who had previously self-injured measurably relaxed whilst they imagined self-injury, whilst the 'control' group of people who had not previously deliberately injured themselves did not – they became more stressed.

As counsellors, we draw on our own emotional experience – knowing how something has felt for us, or how we imagine it might feel – when empathising with clients. Having experienced something similar, or being able to imagine doing so, enables us to get somewhere alongside our client and only becomes a problem when we slip into thinking that the client's experience must be the *same* as our own, as opposed to it being similar to our own. Counsellors who have never deliberately injured themselves in order to calm down, and do not calm down at the thought of doing so, will not have their own embodied experience to draw on when trying empathically to understand a client who self-harms for this reason. We can accept that our client's experience is as they say, and that it is different from our own, but this falls short of empathic understanding. However, theoretical understanding can be a source of empathic understanding if it enables us to imagine an experience, and fortunately there is a wealth of recent research that can help us imagine the relief some people get from injuring themselves.

Hyper-Arousal

A great many people who deliberately injure themselves have had extreme and obviously traumatic experiences, such as physical or sexual abuse, and abuse is often understood to be an indicator of self-injury in the future. However, many people who have been sexually or physically abused do not self-injure. Research indicates that emotional neglect – what has *not* been done rather than what has been done – seems to be the most reliable predictor of self-injury (Van der Kolk et al., 1991). People who self-injure are very likely to have been emotionally neglected as children or to have suffered a significant separation from their main carer. Even young monkeys who are parted from their mothers self-injure.

Why might emotional neglect in childhood predispose someone to injure themselves in later life? Although deliberate self-injury is rarely mentioned in such literature, there is a growing body of research from developmental psychology and neuroscience that suggests some useful answers. This research demonstrates that brain development, specifically the right-hand side of the brain, which enables us to calm down when we are emotionally overstimulated, is dependent on the quality of our earliest relationship. Babies who are not met with loving and empathic care-giving do not become able, as adults, to regulate their own feelings; in other words, they cannot choose to calm down when stressed.

Comment

This research emphasises the importance of visual stimulus in evoking an emotional response (Schore, 2003b), and so I suggest that in your mind's eye you imagine a very young baby, a baby who is hungry, uncomfortable, scared or in pain. All the baby can do about it is cry. The baby's face will become distorted with tension, its skin will flush, its whole body will become tense – it will display all the signs of heightened physiological arousal.

Perhaps you can feel your own body respond as you imagine this. You may feel tension mounting within yourself and experience an embodied urge to comfort the imaginary baby, and so dissipate the tension within yourself and the baby.

This urge is deeply trustworthy. Contemporary collaborative research between developmental psychologists and neuroscientists provides 'hard' scientific evidence that human growth is an intersubjective event. The brain is one of the least developed organs in a new baby and develops (or not) in response to how the baby is responded to during particular periods of development in early infancy.

'Hard' science is recognising that a child's psychological development is dependent on contact, attention, loving acceptance and empathic responses. Of course this is also a basic tenet of PCT theory. PCT is often characterised as being WASPy (white Anglo-Saxon Protestant), individualistic and emphasising of autonomy and independence rather than interdependence. Those values are strongly present in white North American culture, and so it is hardly surprising that they are present in Rogers' work. However, there is also another thread in Rogers' work that is about the fundamental necessity of relationship. Nurturing relationship – sufficiently consistent contact, unconditional acceptance and empathic understanding – is essential to the organism's psychological development, and the absence of such a relationship is damaging. The new research confirms PCT theory, but also challenges it. Rogers conceived of the organismic self as self-regulating. It seems that in the light of contemporary research, the organism's ability to self-regulate, physiologically and psychologically, is not a given, but develops as a result of genuine contact, acceptance and empathy.

If we put the research into neural development alongside the research that shows emotional neglect in childhood to be the most common denominator amongst people who self-injure, we can arrive at a deeper understanding of why people injure themselves in order to calm down. A baby's biological and psychological stress responses do not work in harmony with each other. If the parent (the term 'carer' or 'significant other' would be equally appropriate) changes a distressed baby's nappy one need may be taken care of, but a baby cannot 'tell' its body to calm down once it has what it needs. The baby will probably not stop crying unless it is also soothed. Soothing – gentle, loving attention, stroking, patting, gazing, smiling and baby talk – is as important as changing or feeding the baby. It is this embodied interaction that enables the baby's biological process to get into synch with its psychological process (Gunnar and Donzella, 2002). Unless this process of embodied soothing happens often enough, the neural pathways that enable us to regulate the intensity of our feelings do not develop. The baby's mind and body do not start to work in conjunction with each other, and the baby becomes an adult who cannot calm down just because the emergency is over (Schore, 1994, 2003a, 2003c).

As the baby becomes stressed, their brain triggers the production of various chemicals, including the hormone cortisol (Yehuda, 1999). Cortisol helps us deal more effectively with stressful situations by helping us to focus all our resources. It does this by shutting down other systems, like the immune system, and our relaxation and learning processes (Chambers et al., 1999; McEwen, 1999). As the baby is soothed, its cortisol level drops, and its immune, learning and relaxation systems are restored.

If a crying baby is habitually ignored, treated coldly or not soothed and comforted by being held and patted or stroked, its system becomes flooded with cortisol, and if this happens often, its cortisol receptors, which mop up cortisol, close down. When the baby's cortisol level rises in response to stress in the future, there are not enough receptors to absorb it (Caldji et al., 2000). Cortisol flooding the hippocampus can affect its growth (Lyons et al., 2000). If this happens, then the child's memory and ability to learn will also be compromised. Although we are particularly vulnerable to this damage in the hippocampus as babies, cortisol receptors can also close down in adults experiencing long-term stress. Disabled cortisol receptors make the hippocampus less sensitive to cortisol, and this interrupts the process by which it tells the hypothalamus to stop ordering cortisol production. Cortisol levels continue to rise, which can lead to neuron loss in the hippocampus. Just as the neural pathways in a baby's brain may fail to develop because its parent fails to regulate its stress levels through loving and empathic contact, so parts of an adult's brain may atrophy as a result of long-term stress (Collins and Depue, 1992; Konyecsni and Rogeness, 1998).

Imagine

So, imagine feeling really stressed about something, and doing whatever normally works for you – talking to someone about how you feel, rationalising, working out a strategy, and so on – and for that just to make no difference. Imagine this always being the case. Imagine being simply unable to calm down.

Some readers will be able to imagine this very easily, as a dis-unified stress response is by no means uncommon. However, counsellors who do not experience this process may fail to recognise that a client does. A client, whom I will call Keir, helped me to recognise it.

Keir I

Keir frequently became very anxious, and was, at the time, horribly anxious about something that was extremely unlikely to happen. As we carefully explored the situation she was worried about, she was able to notice, and me to hear, that in fact her mind had stopped racing and that the catastrophising flights of fear had stopped. She knew that her imagined catastrophe really was very unlikely to happen, and knew what she would do if it did. I checked out my impression that her mind seemed settled, and she confirmed that it was and that she was no longer worried about the situation. She paused, looked slightly puzzled, and said, 'but my heart is still racing'.

We had found a paradoxical nuance that we had missed previously, largely because I had not been sufficiently sensitised to the range of possible degrees of dis-unity to catch it. Keir illustrated psychological and physiological dis-unity for me, but in order to see it, I had to have some idea of what it was I was looking at. Once I understood that mind-body synchronisation is something that needs to develop, and can therefore fail to develop, I was able to spot its absence. Understanding the developmental theory enabled me to become aware of the fact that Keir was describing a state of dis-unity beyond my own experience, and it also enabled me to imagine what it might be like to experience such dis-unity.

As well as showing that self-injury calms some people down, but not others, Haines et al.'s study (1995) showed that deliberate self-injury relieved physiological stress very quickly indeed – sometimes before the subject began to feel better psychologically. The authors conclude that,

'This result suggests that it is the alteration of psychophysiological arousal that may operate to reinforce and maintain the behaviour, not the psychological response' (Haines et al., 1995: 481). In other words, self-injury reduces physiological stress before the person even starts to feel better psychologically, as the following exchange shows.

Keir II

'I felt so awful after he stood me up,' my client explained. 'I just went home, took out my razor blades and started on my legs again. I felt better after that.'
'You felt better after you'd cut your legs?'
'No. Yes. I still felt bad – really bad, but calm bad.'

The (very scant) research so far (Haines et al., 1995; Sachsse et al., 2002) confirms the subjective reports of many of those who deliberately harm themselves in order to relieve stress. Sachsse et al. (2002), who measured cortisol levels before and after an episode of self-injury, conclude that deliberate self-harm may be regarded as an effective means of gaining control over an otherwise uncontrollable stress response and of regulating hyper-arousal and/or dissociative states.

That self-injury can be shown to lower cortisol levels tells us that self-injury *does* indeed relieve stress, but as cortisol production is a response to stress, and not a cause of stress, it does not tell us *how* deliberate self-injury helps some people to calm down. It has been suggested that self-injury may be so effective because our bodies release endorphins that are thought to act as natural painkillers and produce a feeling of well-being following an injury. However, more research needs to be done in order to understand what chemical responses are involved in deliberate self-injury, particularly as Haines et al.'s (1995) research shows that the biofeedback response to their group of people who had previously self-harmed was no different to the control group when they imagined *accidental* injury.

The research so far suggests that self-harm is, in keeping with the actualising tendency, a means to self-maintenance. It creates greater internal congruence and integration in a person who is unusually dis-integrated, by regulating their physiological stress response. Given that in doing so it regulates the overproduction of cortisol, self-injury possibly protects against brain damage in people who have experienced, or are experiencing, long-term stress. Many people who self-harm have no cognitive understanding of why they do so, but their organism knows what they can do to re-establish internal congruence. Haines et al.'s (1995) study also showed that physiological stress was lowered in those who said that they self-injured for reasons other than to calm down. Whatever a client may be aware of as their reason for injuring themselves, it is worth bearing in mind that they may also be regulating an otherwise out-of-control stress response.

Issues for Practice

People who were treated violently, roughly, coldly or with indifference as children have often learned to be very sensitive to the quality of another person's presence and feel very easily invaded or abandoned. If the counsellor's presence is not very, very gentle such a client is likely to feel threatened and to remain stressed even after the perceived threat has passed. Yet such clients need a very solid presence. The gentleness must not be psychological absence in disguise. The counsellor must be solidly and warmly there in a very gentle way. Being engaged and relaxed, rather than engaged and focused is probably a good place to start. Of course, no general guidelines suit all individuals – the important thing is that the therapist is aware that the quality of their presence is likely to have a particularly strong impact on clients who self-injure in order to calm themselves, and that this can be reflected on in sessions and in supervision.

> **Keir III**
>
> I recently got the quality of my presence wrong for Keir. I had run over with the previous client, who had been doing some very deep work. Normally I potter around for a quarter of an hour between sessions, and this enables me to return to 'neutral' before I see the next person, but, on this occasion, I didn't have time to potter. I was not perturbed by my lack of a break, as I still felt energised and focused. However, I was far too energised and focused for Keir. I sat down, leant forward slightly, focused my attention on her and waited for her to begin. She found this much, much too intense. She felt pressurised to say something by my expectant posture, and invaded by my eagerness to engage. Fortunately, our relationship was such that she was able to tell me so and ask me to 'back off'.

Clients whose psychological and biological processes are out of synch spend much of their energy struggling to establish some inner equilibrium, and really do need to go at their own pace. It may take time for them to connect to how they feel, and once connected they may need to tread very carefully to avoid becoming over-aroused and overwhelmed. Empathic understanding must involve understanding the intensity of a client's experience and their ability to regulate themselves – or not. Trying to help a client be 'more in touch with their feelings' can easily lead to the client being overwhelmed. Keir becomes very easily overwhelmed by her feelings, and focusing on them for too long can leave her hyper-aroused for days. She needs to pace herself very carefully indeed in order to avoid going into a state in which she feels that she needs to harm herself. Keir says that the only thing that calms her down is chatting with me. Our chat is not simply avoidance. Sitting together and talking about something non-stirring and inconsequential enables Keir to use my embodied presence to help calm her physiolog-ical stress.

Keir IV

'I'm feeling really tense again today. My body feels totally rigid with holding all the distress. My back hurts. I don't want to talk about anything that will make me feel – I'd just get overwhelmed.'
'I wonder what would help? Do you have a sense of what you need to do today?'
'I just want to sit here by the fire and chat. I can't cope with any more than that.'
'You sound like you need to be soothed. Do you want that furry blanket?'
'Yes, and can you sit closer to me?'
'Sure. Did you watch that film last night? The one set in Newcastle?'
'I thought the scene where they have a day out in the country was hilarious.'
'Yeah, and when they all go to that woman's house ... '

Chatting at length with clients is something that is generally frowned upon, and it is certainly important that when we are working with a client we are working therapeutically and not just lapsing into something that is essentially not much different from social contact. The client should be getting something that they could not get from a social relationship. If I found myself chatting with another client, I might wonder if we were avoiding something: if we might be having problems recognising that the therapy was over, or if I was neglecting the boundaries of the therapeutic relationship in some other way. Chatting is close to the boundary between therapy and friendship. It is my responsibility, as the therapist, to make sure that our relationship remains that of client/counsellor.

My chats with Keir are always about her, or something neutral like a television programme. I am 'me' when we chat – I have opinions on the TV programmes and so on – but our chats are not *about* me. Keir needs me to be her therapist, not her friend.

Whatever Keir and I may be chatting about, I believe that our bodies are getting on with important work. I am clear that our chatting has a thera-peutic aim, so I am relaxed about it, and Keir's breathing becomes slower and her posture more relaxed, partly in response to mine, just as a baby is soothed by the relaxed presence of a parent.

Not only does my body enable her body to calm down in the moment, but – hopefully – our contact will, over time, help make permanent changes in Keir's biological stress response, bringing it into a closer relationship with her psychological response. As a child Keir was denied a contactful, empathic and unconditionally loving primary relationship in which she felt secure and safe. She was not soothed when she was distressed and does not have the ability to soothe herself now. Keir really cannot calm down when an emergency is over, and in her world most things are an emergency. The neural pathways in her brain that would enable her to moderate the intensity of her feelings do not exist.

My therapeutic task is to help them form. Unless a child is so severely neglected that the necessary neurons die (as with the children in Romanian orphanages who sustained permanent brain damage), his or her brain remains capable of growth. Trustworthy relationships in later life offer the potential for more positive experiences and the formation of new neural pathways. Unconditional acceptance makes the relationship secure, but empathic understanding is important too. Empathic understanding is not, as Rogers describes it, purely cognitive. It involves not only understanding the client's feelings in the context of their inner world, but also *sensing* them as if they were one's own. My empathy must be as congruent as my acceptance. Keir needs to *see*, not just hear, that I understand what she feels. And she needs to see that I can experience those feelings without fear, that I can experience them without becoming overwhelmed.

If Keir has become stressed by her contact with me, and is keeping me at a psychological and physical distance, it becomes very important to her to be able to hold one of my cats. I have several cats, and Keir is fond of all of them, but if she needs to soothe herself, she chooses a particularly languid cat, who seeks psychological contact through leaning her relaxed body into Keir's, and gazing at her. In other words, my cat does what Keir's mother presumably did not. She uses her physical presence to make psychological contact, and to soothe, when words are not possible. My cat may well be helping Keir change her biochemical stress response by soothing her in such an embodied way.

When she is not keeping me at a distance, Keir sometimes asks me to soothe her in an embodied way – usually to stroke her head or hold her hand. However, therapeutic touch is an infinitely trickier business for you or me than it is for a cat. People who have been treated violently, roughly or coldly as babies, or whose parents did not respond to the 'I've had enough now – I need some space' signals that babies give, often feel very easily invaded as adults. Sometimes this is because they became so used to their boundaries being invaded that they have lost all sense of what does or does not feel comfortable. Sometimes it is because they are very wary of other people, and can easily experience contact as threatening, or just too 'full on'. Sometimes it is because they do not give themselves permission to say, or even be aware, that the contact feels too close. Often it is for all of these reasons. I am not referring to sexualised contact, or even contact that the client misinterprets as sexualised. Touch that feels uncomfortable, even if it is not experienced as sexual, is damaging because it is just not what the client wants.

Feeling that we have choice and control over how close other people come or who touches us, and how, is vital to our basic sense of safety in the world. People who have had experience of hostile or unwelcome contact, especially as children, often do not have this basic sense of safety, and feel invaded and threatened very easily indeed. Because the experience of feeling invaded involves a sense of choice being taken away, of a sense of dis-empowerment and often of helplessness, it becomes even harder for the client to say that they want the therapist to stop.

I make sure that Keir asks for any physical contact we have, including how close she wants me to sit that particular day, and that she is specific about me stroking her head or putting my hand on her shoulder. I have, on a few occasions, found myself putting my hand on her arm in a spontaneous gesture of comfort, but have noticed that I do so in slow motion, checking with Keir as I do, whether it is okay or not. I would pull back if I got anything less than a positive affirmation – absence of reaction is not necessarily permission. Touch is a complete 'no-no' for many therapists because it is so risky. It is certainly not something to do if you feel uncomfortable or anxious about doing it as this will be communicated in the quality of your touch, and defeat the purpose. It is wise, if you do touch clients, to make sure that there is a *continuous* dialogue going on about what is, or is not, comfortable.

For many clients, simply being in another person's warm and relaxed presence is sufficient physical contact. I find that the clients who have been abused or neglected the most severely and who self-harm the most seriously find it enough (and any more would be too much) just to sit with me in silence, slowly getting used to being in another person's presence without fear. Some clients need to do this for many sessions, or large portions of many sessions, before they are ready to do anything else.

The quality of a therapist's absence is as important as the quality of their presence; and this may be particularly true for clients who self-harm in order to reduce stress and who are using therapy to establish a sense of safety-in-relationship.

Keir V

'So, it's been three weeks since we've seen each other. I'm wondering how it was for you while I was on holiday?'

'Well I missed – lots. I saw the colleague you'd recommended a couple of times and that helped a bit, but I may not bother next time.'

'Because that only helped a bit or ... '

'This time I knew you'd come back.'

'So you didn't feel so anxious?'

'No, I didn't. You can go on holiday again if you like – but not until next year!'

'Cheers. That's good of you. Seriously though, this has happened very gradually, but it's such a change. I remember when you used to see someone else and have phone sessions with me if I was working away.'

'Yes, and I'd still find the separation utter torture.'

'Yes, and you'd be *incandescently* furious with me when I came back.'

'I'm furious with you now. But I also know you need to go away sometimes. It's sort of okay.'

This movement towards needing my – or another therapist's – actual physical presence less has been a very important piece of developmental work for Keir. Because she was not sufficiently soothed by her mother as a child, but was subjected to verbal violence, she did not develop much ability to trust other people. Not only has Keir managed to develop trust in me, but also she has moved through a period of high dependence to a place from which a more abstract idea that I am there is almost as soothing as my actual physical presence. She knows that I am 'there', even when I am not in the same room, or even in the same country.

Keir has learned that I have not abandoned her by leaving, and that my temporary absence is tolerable. Whereas Keir would, in the past, cut herself a great deal if I were unable to see her, she now only cuts occasionally. She is, very slowly, becoming more able to regulate her own stress response without self-harming.

Conclusion

Research shows that self-injury reduces physiological stress, whether or not that particular person cites stress reduction as the reason for their self-harm. It also shows that there is a time lag between physiological stress being lowered, and the person who is self-harming actually feeling better. Both of these discoveries suggest that many people who self-harm are regulating their internal state, but may be unaware that they are doing so. It is worth keeping this possibility in mind when working with someone who gives other reasons for hurting themselves.

It is important that we take particular care in working with clients who self-harm in order to regulate overwhelming stress or a dissociated state. Research into emotional and neurological development shows that a deficiency of love, attention, acceptance and empathy during certain windows of growth affects our future ability to regulate our feelings. It seems likely that a great many people who self-harm have suffered neglect, resulting in a physiological stress response that is easily triggered, but not easily regulated. Work with these clients needs to be slow and careful if it is to be helpful rather than overstimulating.

Guide to Further Reading

Gerhardt, S. (2004) *Why Love Matters*. Hove: Brunner-Routledge.

An excellent and accessible introduction to findings from neuroscience regarding the importance of early relationships in development.

Sachsse, U., von der Heyde, S. and Huethe, G. (2002) 'Stress regulation and self-mutilation', *American Journal of Psychiatry*, 159 (4): 672.

Puts the case for deliberate self-injury as purposeful behaviour.

Spandler, H. and Warner, S. (2007) *Beyond Fear and Control: Working with Young People who Self-Harm*. Ross-on-Wye: PCCS Books.

A collection of chapters commissioned by an agency that works with young people. There is a strong focus on issues of power and oppression in most chapters. In it, an earlier version of this chapter (i.e. 'A Person-Centred Perspective on Self-Injury'), and another by Teres Fickl, directly address practice issues for counsellors.

Many of the texts listed in the **References** section will also be helpful.

References

Alderman, T. (1997) *The Scarred Soul: Understanding and Ending Self-inflicted Violence*. Oakland, CA: New Harbinger.

Caldji, D., Doirio, J. and Meaney, M (2000) 'Variations in maternal care in infancy regulate the development of stress reactivity', *Biological Psychiatry*, 48: 1164–74.

Chambers, R.A., Bremmer, J., Moghaddam, B., Southwick, S., Charney, D. and Krystal, J. (1999) 'Glutamate and PDSD', *Seminars in Clinical Neuropsychiatry*, 4 (4): 274–81.

Collins, P. and Depue, R. (1992) 'A neurobehavioural systems approach to developmental psycopathology: Implications for disorders of affect', in D. Cicchetti and S. Toth (eds), *Rochester Symposium on Developmental Psychopathology*, vol. 4. Rochester, NY: Rochester University Press, pp. 29–102.

Gunnar, M. and Donzella, B. (2002) 'Social regulation of the cortisol levels in early human development', *Psychoneuroendocrinology*, 27: 199–220.

Favazza, A.R. (1996) *Bodies Under Siege: Self-Mutilation and Body Modification in Culture and Psychiatry*. Baltimore, MD: Johns Hopkins University Press.

Favazza, A.R. and Rosenthal, R.J. (1993) 'Diagnostic issues in self-mutilation', *Hospital and Community Psychiatry*, 44: 134–40.

Haines, J., Williams, C.L., Brain, K.L. and Wilson, G.V. (1995) 'The psychophysiology of self-mutilation', *Journal of Abnormal Psychology*, 104 (3): 471–89.

Klonsky, D. (2007) 'The functions of deliberate self-injury: A review of the evidence', *Clinical Psychology Review*, 27: 226–39.

Konyecsni, G.M. and Rogeness, G. (1998) 'The effects of early social relationships on neurotransmitter development and the vulnerability to affective disorders', *Seminars in Clinical Neuropsychiatry*, 3 (4): 285–301.

Lyons, D., Lopez, J., Yang, C. and Schatzberg, A. (2000) 'Stress level corti-sol treatment impairs inhibitory control of behaviour in monkeys', *Journal of Neuroscience*, 20 (20): 7816–21.

McEwen, B. (1999) 'Lifelong effects of hormones on brain development', in L. Schmidt and J. Schulkin (eds), *Extreme Fear, Shyness and Social Phobia*. Oxford: Oxford University Press, pp. 173–98.

Rogers, C.R. (1951) *Client-Centered Therapy: Its Current Practice, Implications, and Theory*. Boston, MA: Houghton Mifflin.

Sachsse, U., von der Heyde, S. and Huether, G. (2002) 'Stress regulation and self-mutilation', *American Journal of Psychiatry*, 159 (4): 672.

Schore, A.N. (1994) *Affect Regulation and the Origin of the Self: The Neuro-biology of Emotional Development*. Hillsdale, NJ: Erlbaum.

Schore, A.N. (2003a) *Affect Regulation and Disorders of the Self*. New York: Norton.

Schore, A.N. (2003b) *Affect Dysregulation and Disorders of the Self*. New York: Norton.

Schore, A.N. (2003c) *Affect Regulation and the Repair of the Self*. New York: Norton.

Suyemoto, K.L. (1998) 'The functions of self-mutilation', *Clinical Psychology Review*, 18 (5): 531–54.

Turp, M. (2003) *Hidden Self-Harm: Narratives from Psychotherapy*. London: Jessica Kingsley Publishers.

Van der Kolk, B., Perry, C. and Herman, J. (1991) 'Childhood origins of self-destructive behaviour', *American Journal of Psychiatry*, 148 (12): 1665–71.

Yehuda, R. (1999) 'Linking the neuroendocrinology of post-traumatic stress disorder with recent neuroanatomic findings', *Seminars in Clinical Neuropsychiatry*, 4: 256–65.

11

PERSON-CENTRED THERAPY IN PRACTICE

PAUL WILKINS AND JANET TOLAN

The Importance of Theory

In our introductory chapter and throughout this book the importance of a thorough grounding in person-centred theory to person-centred practice has been emphasised. However, as Sheila Haugh so eloquently puts it in her chapter on bereavement, it is vital that this theory be 'held lightly'. In other words, the person in the client role is at the centre of person-centred practice – theory informs practice but does not dictate it. By this we do not mean that, as person-centred practitioners, we have licence to indulge personal eccentricities, idiosyncrasies and whims (especially not those based on a misunderstanding of what it means to be congruent). Rather we mean that, as we practise, our full attention should be on our client, and our effort should be to understand the world of the client as it is perceived, and not on trying to fit the person and the 'problem' to theory. Again, Sheila Haugh told us of the importance of models of bereavement process as guides or approximations and that they are not rigid, linear, necessary routes to healing. To assume that the bereaved client in front of you is engaged in a process exactly the same as you may have read about it in a book or heard about it in a lecture and act accordingly would be a mistake. This is especially true when you take into account the cultural background of your client. This involves more than obvious differences in ethnicity, religious practice, class and so on. It may be that a client who you assign to a similar cultural group as yourself has different family traditions that impinge on the way that grief is experienced, expressed and processed.

So, it is the job of the therapist dealing with a bereaved client to pay attention to the experience of grief and loss *as the client expresses (or does not express) it*, not as theory tells you.

Of course, as is evident from the other chapters in the book, what applies to grief applies to trauma, childhood abuse, depression, anxiety, experiencing different realities, issues with drugs and alcohol, difficulties with food and a predilection to self-injure. This, for example, explains Kirshen Rundle's resistance to labels and diagnoses when dealing with clients who are 'depressed' or whose experience and perception of the world is very different from her own. It is also true of all the other presenting issues you may encounter in the course of your practice. Another thing to remember is that a lot of reactions to life events we encounter in the therapy room are normal. As Kirshen Rundle points out, it is not unusual for human beings to be miserable from time to time (for example, when bereaved or having experienced loss of other kinds); Allan Turner makes it apparent that anxiety is an expected reaction to being traumatised, and Richard Bryant-Jefferies reiterates this. So, it is unnecessary to 'pathologise' reactions to life events.

From a person-centred perspective, our actualising tendencies prompt us to do the best that we can in response to the world as we experience it. Feelings of discomfort are sometimes necessary precursors to the process of change and growth. This means that (for example) depression is not always best dealt with by combatting it. Sometimes an exploration of the experience and its meaning is more helpful. This is true also of issues with food and eating, although Barbara Douglas makes it clear that there are issues of the client's safety to consider too – using drugs and alcohol or self-injury. As harmful and as aberrant as these reactions appear to be, Rose Cameron and Barbara Douglas tell us of the importance of seeing things from the client's perspective and accepting them and what they do rather than rushing headlong into attempts to counteract the particular behaviour. People have reasons for doing what they do and it may be that it is not until these are understood and accepted that change is possible.

The Centrality of the Actualising Tendency, Self-Structure and Self-Concept

As you read what the experienced practitioners who have contributed to this book have to say about their work, you will notice that they all attribute the process of growth and healing to their clients' actualising tendencies and not to their own expertise or techniques. They facilitate their clients' actualising process; and their knowledge of (for example) anxiety, difficulties with food and eating, or using drugs and alcohol helps them to do this. This is axiomatic to person-centred practice and leads inexorably to the principle of non-directivity.

Moreover, it emphasises the importance of responding to each person as unique and with a unique experience of the world. That is to say, each of us has a particular self-structure, self-concept and ideal self. This too is evident from the chapters in this book. This means that (for example), no two people respond in exactly the same way to being bereaved – see Sheila Haugh's story of Andrew and his 'different' reaction to loss – or, as Allan Turner makes clear, to being involved in a traumatic incident. However, each author is also very clear that knowledge of what *may* be the experience of people who come to them presenting the issue they are writing about is helpful to both the practitioner and the client. However, as Kirshen Rundle points out, what is really important is understanding the client's frame of reference. Thus, as Jane Power says, understanding that conditions of worth resulting from childhood sexual abuse will have in some way shaped the (incongruent) self-structure of the adult who experienced such abuse, and who is now in the client's chair, is essential to successful work with that person.

Person-Centred Practice with People Reacting to Life Events

All the contributors to this book state in some way or another what you might think is obvious. Regardless of the presenting issue the client brings, the right and proper way to be in response to them is to offer the therapist-provided conditions (that is, to be congruent, empathic and to have unconditional positive regard for them). It is also evident that without the presence of the other three necessary and sufficient conditions – (psychological) contact, the vulnerability or anxiety of the client, and that the client perceives the empathy and unconditional positive regard of the therapist – steps to constructive change will be few if any. How then does the specialist knowledge each tells us about apply?

One way of looking at this is to see that it facilitates the congruence, empathy and unconditional positive regard of the therapist. It is only when we understand something of how the client might feel (or not feel) in response to what they have experienced, and are able to accept that what on the face of it looks like damaging or even deplorable behaviour – is, in some way (however distorted) – constructive or protective, that we can fully empathise and accept the other. It is only when we can see the person beyond their manifest incongruence arising from distortion, denial, an external locus of evaluation and their conditions of worth, that we can be a companion on their sometimes painful journey towards growth. It is knowledge of the what, why and wherefore of things that can help us do this. We can learn this from tales of successful practice (as in the vignettes with which all the contributors illustrate their accounts), and sometimes by considering contributions to theoretical understanding from other quarters is helpful. This is why, for instance, Allan Turner tells us something about other understandings of critical incident response and trauma; Jane Power cites research into the experience of childhood sexual abuse; Barbara Douglas explains a variety of models used in the understanding of eating difficulties; and Rose Cameron draws on the evidence from neuroscience and psychophysiological research to explain the effects of self-injury.

Reactions to Life Events are Rarely Simple

All the contributors to this book make it clear that, whatever aspect of the experience of life events they are writing about, there are links to others. Although clients and referrers may present issues as 'unipolar' – 'I am depressed', 'This client has an eating disorder', 'I remember something awful happening to me when I was a kid' – it would be extremely unusual if that were the sole factor. This means that it would be a mistake to focus on and 'treat' the presenting issue to the exclusion of all other things. For example, Richard Bryant-Jefferies says that sometimes a presenting issue of 'anxiety' turns out to be rooted in 'forgotten' childhood sexual abuse and that extreme states of anxiety and panic can link to the experience of altered realities (psychoses); Barbara Douglas is clear that eating difficulties can arise from a variety of life experiences; and Rose Cameron tells us that the urge to self-injure is associated with neglect and an absence of empathy. So, whatever your client brings as a presenting issue, it is likely that something else will be going on too. For example, a bereaved person may very well be 'depressed' (perhaps 'sad' or even 'miserable' would be a better word) because grief and loss of any kind bring sorrow, but equally and perhaps at the same time they may be anxious. The anxiety might arise from a fear that they will not cope without the person they have lost or it might be anxiety arising from incongruence – perhaps the self-structural belief that there is no point in dwelling on painful things. They may have problems with eating or have taken to using alcohol or drugs to help them get by. Similarly, someone who experiences panic attacks may hear voices or suffer hallucinations and doubt their sanity. For those whose self-structure categorises mad people as risible or inferior, this may be understandably hard to admit.

It is not beyond the realms of possibility that you could be presented with a client to whom every chapter in this book is relevant. However, there would be no need to panic. Informed by the knowledge that our contributors have shared with you, and aware of the importance of keeping the client and the client's frame of reference to the fore while you consistently offer the therapist-provided conditions, neither your client nor you is likely to come to harm.

Finally ...

We think that by now you will understand that to be an effective practitioner what you need to do is to make sure that you inform yourself about the kinds of issues clients bring to therapy and to ground yourself thoroughly in theory. This will help you to become more accepting of what you are told by your client and what you witness (although supervision and personal development work also have a part to play). If you do this and then 'hold lightly' that theory and knowledge, putting understanding and responding to your client's perception at the heart of your practice, you will be helpful to your clients.

INDEX